I0411303

(1)

Education was circulated among common people in some pockets on earth, and it was not so circulated in other pockets though subject matter of education or knowledge was known to some sections of people in those areas. It is a mystery and beyond our sphere of comprehension why there was difference in custom among different areas. We find production and circulation of few articles of most primary stage among groups of people who still remain in primitive condition wherever they exist on earth. Everywhere we find circulation and usage of such most primary stage articles like earthen bowl and dish, stone made blunt weapons and after that metallic spears, bows and arrows, swords, daggers and axes etc wherever such primitive people exist on earth – be it in India, Africa, America or Australia. We find similarities of behaviour among these people in few other respects – all these people have no education and they exist in primitive style. Probably primitive people living at different places independently invented most primary articles like stone made blunt weapons, earthen utensils etc without taking help of people in other places. These articles might have not been invented at certain particular locations on earth to circulate thereafter production processes of such articles all over the world. We find circulation of such articles among people living in distant islands who have no contact with any civilized people outside. So it is not very difficult to guess that primitive people living at different places on earth independently invented such articles without help of people outside. And we have to take into consideration another factor, no extra acquired knowledge was required for invention and regular production of such most primary articles. Humankind could invent and produce such articles with the help of basic instincts and intuitions. Level of basic instincts and intuition of all people all over the world is equal.

There is no difference among people living at different places in terms of basic instincts and intuitions, people living at Africa or Greenland or Japan have equal level of instincts. Only extra acquired knowledge makes people at different places different when knowledge is introduced and circulated among people at certain particular places. Some people are better educated and intelligent to perform jobs, other people are less educated.

Number of such most primary articles which primitive people could invent and produce with the help of basic instincts and intuitions was very few. No one in human society felt any trouble to learn production processes of all such articles. All members of society used to join in production of such articles and they used to divide produced articles equally among themselves. There was no difference in acquired wealth and idea of private property did not appear in human society as all people were able to produce all things and used to divide equally among themselves. There was no dispute quarrel or brawl among people in relation to private property, nor any theft or robbery. Even now we do not find offences like theft robbery etc. among primitive people wherever they are living scattered on earth, so they do not feel need of administration.

There is probably nothing wrong that human beings feel attracted to artificial articles. Even many inferior creatures are eager to use artificial articles. Weaving birds can build very beautiful nests, thrush and dove also build small beautiful nests. Fox, wild pig, hare etc. dig hole in earth to live therein. They are not just ready to remain satisfied with natural materials endowed by nature; they are capable to prepare something else utilizing such materials available in nature in natural conditions. When humankind appeared on earth, they also joined the group to produce artificial articles moulding natural materials. Man was devoid of sharp teeth and nail, but they had to encounter wild animals for both collecting food and self defense. They manufactured blunt stone made weapons. Probably invention of articles initiated among humankind with blunt weapons, that was the beginning. Thereafter one after other appeared thatched huts made of branches and leaves, ignition of fire, earthen utensils and many others. Every member in human society used to consume and enjoy all articles produced with the help of basic instincts and intuitions, it was not probable that some members of society would use such articles and others would avoid those. All members in human society in distant past, irrespective of difference of age and position in society, used to consume such articles whatever was in circulation in human society during that time. There was no division in human society like Brahmins and non Brahmin, higher and lower castes at that time during initial stage of human civilisation and they did not show any difference in nature in consumption of articles. No one was deprived to procure and consume any article. No custom was prevalent at that time so that some people were entitled to consume and enjoy articles while others used to just stare with eagerness. There were only few consumable articles in vogue among human beings. No one used to find it greatly troublesome to learn production processes of few numbers of articles. As all were equally skilled in production processes of all articles and all used to take part in production of such articles there was no division of profession. Idea of private property did not appear till that time and profession called business did not start among humankind. Need for business or transaction was not felt till that time as everyone could produce his necessary articles. There was no opportunity for anybody to earn extra profit by exploiting others in one's own business or profession in absence of idea of private property. Division of employers and employees or exploiters and exploited was unknown till that time. Similarly there was no opportunity for any class of persons to consume and enjoy more by depriving some other class. Everyone used to divide equally among themselves all produced articles as they used to produce all articles conjointly. There used to be no difference of more or less among members. That time population was less among human race all over the world as rate of increase of population was low. Population increase happened when patriarchal system became prevalent among mankind on account of circulation of large number of artificial articles. Civilized society – where large number of artificial articles were invented and circulated, and women of society were unable to join such jobs on account of laborious nature of production process of such articles, for which patriarchal system became a formidable custom – was fertile source of population explosion. We need not go very far in search of evidences to prove this point. We have sufficient strong evidences which happened within few centuries of our time. The Spanish captured all civilized areas of both of Americas which were spread in southern part of northern America and north western part of South America. There were many thriving cities and towns in these widespread areas of both Americas. Knowledge was revealed among Maya Inca and Aztec and that knowledge was circulated among ordinary people. These civilised nations saw progress of material civilisation, large number of artificial articles were invented and circulated among them but women were denied opportunity to participate in jobs on account of laborious nature of production process of articles, women became subjugated to men, patriarchal system became dominant social order and as a result population increased. Even plague epidemic used to outbreak frequently among them in their populous cities and towns and large number of people used to be decimated as a result. Plague epidemic happens probably as a consequence of population explosion. This epidemic happens when there is deficiency of clean food and drink on account of population explosion. Material civilisation progressed to a significant extent in civilized areas of both of Americas and along with that patriarchy was established, and population also increased. There were widespread jungles outside civilized areas in both of Americas where primitive nations used to live in small groups, scattered on a land mass full of jungle, and well away from each other. No knowledge ever revealed among them, particularly that of number system and measurement, and material civilisation did not progress. The Spanish captured all civilised areas of Americas and in the process encountered all oppositions from civilised nations. The English and Portuguese captured lands covered with dense jungles. They did not take as much risk as was undertaken by the Spanish, and were happy capturing wild areas of both of Americas avoiding civilized areas. These two nations reached America after the Spanish. Lands which they captured in both of Americas were full of jungles and were not known to have any populous human habitat. Some persons among invaders from the English and Portuguese who joined initial stage of invasion and capturing of land and settlement of primitive people in both of Americas recorded their experiences and memoirs. Did they mention anywhere that these jungles were full of human habitations? Knowledge did not expose among primitive human groups, material civilisation did not progress and population did not increase. They used to live sparsely and scattered and well away from each other inside dense jungle in primitive condition. Picture was same in Africa. There also primitive tribes used to live in small groups inside dense jungles keeping distance from each other. Such Africans used to be captured and imported in distant past to be engaged as slaves during domination by Romans. Many of them used to be trained to fight as gladiators in coliseum, giving them good food and allowing them to build their physique. There was no change in attitude of Europeans to Africans in last few centuries. Rather slave trade became more intensified. Africans were captured and sold in slave market of both Europe and America. Minority Africans, who used to live in small groups in dense jungles well away from each other, could not form any formidable defense to protect themselves against onslaught of Europeans when they used to attack small villages of Africans in last few centuries inside dense jungles to capture them, and the Africans used to surrender meekly without opposition. So there was no population increase in dark Africa. Comparatively Europe was hugely populous and densely inhabited in her principal cities during same time where there was painful increase of population. Some empirical records of population increase in different continents in last few centuries have been compiled. While population increase in the Europe crossed 500 percent in last few centuries, such increase in the Africa was 40 percent during same time. We do not know whether populations of both of Americas Australia etc. wherever European settlements were built, were taken into consideration in this population increase of Europeans. If European settlers in Americas and other places, who were deported from mainland and land of origin Europe to settle in colonies elsewhere, were not considered earlier to be added in increased population of Europe and are now so added with Europeans, then Europeans increased by at least 2000 percentage in last few centuries. Population increase whatever we find among Africans happened recently, that can be an indication that large number of articles have now been produced and circulated among them and patriarchy has become a dominant social order. Those articles were mostly circulated among Africans by Europeans in last few centuries. There was no such population increase among Africans before circulation of so many articles. Such events do never prove that spread of education checks population increase. Human groups, among whom no knowledge was ever revealed or subject matter of knowledge was never formed, who were or even now are living in primitive condition inside dense jungle, did not increase population or do not so increase even now. Nations, among whom knowledge was revealed and all people were allowed to join process of education – though all people did not join education, particularly those who remained engaged with physically laborious jobs kept themselves away from education or stopped their education at certain early stage – increased in the past and even now they increase population. Here we find some relation between progress of material civilisation and population increase. Population increase happened among those human groups, among whom material civilisation appeared and developed. Which particular feature of material civilisation is cause of population increase? There we find that women in society which has advanced in material civilisation are subjugated and confined. In contrast women among primitive human groups, who did not see progress of material civilisation, are free in movement and are not dependant on anybody. We also find that women do not participate in work in nations who have advanced in material civilisation. And there we can come to learn if we be inquisitive that it is impossible for women to take part in jobs on account of physically laborious nature of production process to produce articles in lands which have experienced progress in material civilisation. Patriarchal system and total dominance over women by men were established as women became thoroughly dependant on men. Also business or transaction started in human society as large numbers of artificial articles were invented produced and circulated. Division of profession happened and everybody was required to select one or two professions as no one could be expected to know production processes of all articles or to take part in production of all articles. Volume of materials produced in one's own business or workshop for exchange or transaction with other articles produced in other professions was subject matter of individual decision. There appeared idea of private property. At certain point of time society decided that men's' own children should inherit their earned and accumulated wealth. Now shame was imposed on women and they were confined behind wall and were restricted from socializing with all men outside to ensure own children of men. Women among primitive societies have full liberty of movement and have no sense of shame and have unrestricted freedom in socializing. But men started showing unreasonable curiosity about women after confining them behind wall. They forgot reason why shame was imposed on women and they were confined behind wall. Combined result of total dominance on women and curiosity about them was population explosion. Population increased at explosive rate in those places where civilisation appeared and progressed and many artificial articles were invented for which patriarchal order became firmly aground on account of labour intensive nature of production process of articles. But all members of any community used to produce all articles conjointly and distribute produced articles equally among themselves as long as numbers of articles were few so that all members did not use to find any difficulty in learning all production processes. Large numbers of articles were not invented till that time, division of profession did not appear in human society and idea of private property was not known. Women at that time used to join men to take part in jobs. Lighter parts of jobs used to be done by women in association with men and heavier and physically laborious parts used to remain assigned to be accomplished by men. Population increase did not happen as long as many articles were not invented and introduced in human society, division of profession did not appear, idea of private property did not come into force and patriarchal order did not become prevalent social custom as women were not altogether incapable and helpless to join jobs till that time. Even now we find such features existing in force among primitive people wherever they are found on earth. No feature like domination exploitation deprivation appeared till that time – how exploitation or deprivation can happen where idea of private property is absent – rather all members used to distribute equally all produced articles among themselves. Also till that time patriarchy did not become dominant social order, and population did not increase in a large scale. Human communities used to live in small groups scattered inside dense jungle well away from each other. There used to be dense and wide jungle, where there used to exist large number of wild animals and fruit bearing trees, surrounding habitat of each human group. Members of any group did not use to toil hard to collect required food for limited number of members of group. So population was low and there was sufficient supply of food. Men did not use to spend much time and energy to collect food. Other jobs in society were very few. They used to enjoy long and enough leisurely time after completing few numbers of jobs in society. This feature of primitive people in distant past during prehistoric time can be substantiated by similar feature present among similar people now wherever they live. How did men use to spend long leisurely time during that dawn of human civilisation when number of articles was few and they used to spend limited time to produce few numbers of articles? Would they join many social and cultural activities? Would they join socializing, games and sports and religious activities? Then we have to admit that men already invented social games and religious activities by that time. That time in human history was a particularly blissful time when men acquired qualities like complete human being, but there was no population increase, only few number of jobs they used to perform as they did not invent large number of articles till that time, sufficient foods were available in surrounding jungles and men used to enjoy long leisurely time after completing few number of jobs. Did human societies join exercise of knowledge and study of nature in some pockets on earth during that long leisurely time, and sphere of knowledge was expanded to a great extent, though they were still living in primitive condition? We can find evidences at many places that everywhere human groups did not advance equally in developing knowledge and intelligence. Many primitive groups are still living on earth. They have very few numbers of jobs among them, few numbers of articles have been invented among them, they enjoy long leisure, but they did not develop much intelligence and knowledge during their stay on earth. They are still living in ignorance. It is a mystery why and how exercise of development of knowledge and intelligence initiated among human beings in few pockets. Did groups of human beings at few places come to unanimous decision while joining social interaction when they had long leisure time that they would join study of nature during that initial stage of human civilisation when human being was still in primitive condition? Anyway it is certain that division of profession did not exist, business and commerce did not become major activity in human society, idea of private property did not come into force, patriarchal order did not become dominant social custom, and population increase did not happen, and there was no exploitation or deprivation in human society till that time, as long as number of artificial articles of consumption was few. All people used to divide things equally among them.

Man always feels curiosity about nature and world. Passing of days and nights, circulation of months and years, change of seasons, change of location of celestial bodies and many other similar phenomena always arouse curiosity in men. Mankind has been studying such natural phenomena from unknown prehistoric time. First knowledge in human society was language and probably the very next was astronomy and simultaneously number system. Long ago in unknown past such knowledge were revealed among humankind. It was surprising that in few of those places where such knowledge was revealed, common people were not allowed to get knowledge. Only people in higher caste, the Brahmins and priests had right to get education, rest of the people in society had no such right, so education did not circulate among those people in lower strata. These Brahmins and priests, among whom knowledge was confined, did not invent and circulate any artificial articles, and common people, who could be possible inventors and producers of articles, were deprived of right to get education. Such human groups did not advance materially. Only those human groups, among whom common people were allowed to get education, saw advancement of material civilisation. We found evidences of revelation of knowledge among people in Harappa Mohenjo-Daro, in west to this in Sumer or Mesopotamia, Assyria, Egypt, sometime later in Greece and Rome, china in the east and outside these centers in both of Americas. There was planned town in Harappa Mohenjo-Daro, brick built houses, roads and public bathing places. Mohenjo-Daro might be world's first planned town, roads were absolutely straight.

Knowledge was exposed among mankind in some places and common people were allowed to learn that knowledge. But all these common people, who were allowed to learn, did not use to join exercise of knowledge with commitment to develop knowledge or reach highest order of knowledge. Most of them used to join education as an urge to perform jobs in profession. Many of them, who were engaged in physically laborious jobs, did not use to join exercise of education and remained ill educated, though centers of education – schools etc – were close to their residences. Many of those who used to join education, used to stop education at certain intermediate stages to utilize their acquired knowledge to invent and produce artificial articles. They did not use to show any eagerness to reach highest order of knowledge or develop and spread knowledge. Artificial articles were invented produced and circulated in the hands of such persons. Of course number system was known and system of measurement was invented among mankind even before that. We can find some articles in common in all human societies all over the world. We find such articles even among those human groups who never saw revelation and advancement of knowledge and intelligence and are still remaining in abysmal darkness of ignorance, and such people never failed to produce such articles during their long stay on earth. Man could invent and produce such primary stage articles at initiation of civilisation by utilizing his elementary instincts and intuition. People living all over the world are same in terms of elementary instincts. Everywhere people invented such articles independently without help from people outside. These articles did not require any extra acquired knowledge for production. That is the reason why such primary stage articles are found everywhere on earth. But men required some extra knowledge, particularly that of number system and measurement for inventing and producing next stage articles. Only those human groups were able to invent and develop next stage articles who came to learn number system and invented system of measurement. Human groups who were unable to learn such knowledge or invent such system were unsuccessful to invent next stage articles and remained in primitive condition. Thereafter human kind invented one by one cart with wheels, brick built houses, wooden furniture and many other articles. Number system and system of measurement are required for inventing such next stage articles. It was therefore not possible for those human groups, among whom number system was not revealed and who did not invent system of measurement, to invent those articles. Many artificial articles were invented among those human groups where ordinary people were allowed to join education and right to join education was not confined in the hands of members of certain particular section of people. Material civilisation or invention and circulation of artificial articles did not progress among those human groups where right to join education used to remain confined in the hands of persons of certain particular section of population, like Brahmin, and members of such section used to join education with certain commitment that they should not discontinue their exercise to acquire knowledge before reaching highest order of knowledge, as we have found in India during Brahmin period when right of education was confined among Brahmins who never utilized their acquired knowledge to invent artificial articles, and for which material civilisation did not progress in India during Brahmin period. Ruins of material civilisation at Harappa Mohenjo-Daro, which flourished 5000 years ago and continued till 1500 year BC, with huge volumes of material evidences are still extant. That civilisation vanished suddenly for unknown reason. Thereafter there was a complete void during next 1000 years, before arrival of Lord Buddha, which is known as Brahmin or Vedic period (both refer to same period). Nobody knows with certainty what happened on Indian soil during that time. We do not find evidence of materials, kings, queens, cities or towns of that period in India. But knowledge was already revealed in India during or before that time as is evident from Vedas, Upanishads and other books of the time. Such books contain evidences of knowledge of mathematics. Also many articles used to be produced during Harappa Mohenjo-Daro civilisation which was not possible without knowledge of number system. It is better to believe that, that knowledge of mathematics was conveyed to and continued during subsequent Vedic period. Knowledge was known in India during that time but only Brahmins were entitled to get education, other non Brahmins were disallowed to learn. Brahmins never invented artificial articles of consumption, their whole time endevour was to reach highest order of knowledge. That is why we do not find evidence of material civilisation of Brahmin period, which was much younger than Harappa Mohenjo-Daro civilisation. This also proves that material civilisation initiated and progressed only there where non Brahmin ordinary people were allowed to get education, but who joined education without commitment to reach highest order of knowledge and ended their education at certain intermediate stage to invent articles of consumption. Similarly material civilisation progressed and artificial articles were invented in those areas among those human groups where all people were allowed to get education but who used to join education without any commitment to reach highest order of knowledge. Of course all people did not use to join education even while enjoying right to get education, particularly those persons who used to remain engaged in physically laborious jobs. Those who were workers, and regularly used to accomplish production processes to produce articles requiring certain knowledge, also required some kind of knowledge as otherwise they could not regularly produce articles. Artificial articles of certain higher stage cannot be produced if we engage some members of primitive people to produce such articles as they are ignorant of certain basic knowledge of production of articles like counting and measurement. Regular engagement of members of civilized people with production of articles is a kind of proof that all people there are entitled to get education. So only those primitive groups of people could join in production of artificial articles in prehistoric time among whom everybody was entitled to get education and they progressed in material civilisation. Some kind of knowledge is required not only for invention of articles but also for regular production, and persons who actually join regular production also require some knowledge. It is certain that material civilisation saw its initiation and progress and some human groups became civilized wherever on earth common people were allowed to get education; and subject matter for initiation and progress of material civilisation, depending on which civilisation started rolling, was known to humankind even before invention of articles. It is certain that material civilisation or invention production and distribution of artificial articles progressed in few pockets on earth being supported by knowledge where common men got right to education. Men required some kind of extra knowledge, particularly that of number system and system of measurement, to invent and produce artificial articles, next to stage of primary articles at very initiation of civilisation whose invention and production did not require any kind of extra acquired knowledge other than elementary instincts and intuitions. Man never halted in invention and production of articles once ball of civilisation started rolling, not even in ancient prehistoric time. It is true that all people who used to join exercise of education did not use to join invention of articles unitedly, very few handful numbers of people used to remain engaged in invention of articles; most of the people used to be engaged in regular production and distribution of articles. Many such artificial articles of consumption continued to be invented and circulated among humankind. It was found at certain point of time that any particular person was unable to learn production processes and produce all kinds of articles which he used to enjoy. Men were eager to consume and enjoy all kinds of articles but it was beyond their capability to learn production processes of all kinds of artificial articles and to join production. There arose division of profession among human beings – smiths, potters, cultivators, carpenters, masons etc. – on account of increase in number of artificial articles, and business or transaction of articles started among them. Everyone was involved in one or two of such professions, but was not satisfied by just enjoying articles produced in one's own profession, and was eager to consume and enjoy articles produced in other professions also. Barter system or system of exchange of articles appeared first. Potters acquired metallic dagger, hoe etc in exchange of own produced earthen pitchers, cauldrons etc, carpenter used to collect bricks in exchange of wooden doors windows etc. Activity called business arose in mankind solely as a result of increase in number of artificial articles when all people were unable to join production of all articles and there arose division of profession. All members of any human society used to lend their hands in production of all articles and distribute produced articles equally among them as long as in ancient age numbers of such articles were low. We find equal distribution of produced articles among primitive people wherever they are living, even in these days, for which there is no more or less of acquired wealth among such people. All of them are equally wealthy with same volume of articles. All members of any primitive group produce and distribute equally among themselves all foods collected, earthen materials and metal made articles like spears, daggers etc. whenever they conjointly produce such articles. Activity called business or transaction did not arise among them as its need was never felt. All members of their community are able to learn and produce few numbers of articles which are in circulation among them. None of them ever fail to take part in production of articles as number of articles is few and everybody can learn production processes of all articles. Everyone can produce articles required by him and does not require to collect any article by means of exchange, so there is no need to join in business or transaction. But thereafter there happened division of profession among those human groups who saw number of articles increased so that no single person was able to learn and produce all articles. Everyone was entitled to decide one's own profession and society had no say in that determination, as everyone had right to determine volume of articles to be produced in one's own profession and volume of other articles to be collected in exchange of own produced articles; society had no right to determine volume of such articles when new artificial articles continued to be invented and division of profession arose as a result of limited capability of men to learn production processes of large number of articles. Many persons could successfully produce and exchange large volume of articles to collect large volume of articles produced in other professions while many others could produce low quantity of articles in their own profession and could collect low quantity of other articles. Some persons were unsuccessful in their profession of production and distribution of articles. Men never agreed to follow any system of sharing their extra acquired wealth with others who had low income. Everyone used to enjoy their own earned wealth. Many persons who failed in any profession or business of production and distribution of articles joined professions of some successful persons as employees and there appeared difference in acquired wealth. But some such unsuccessful persons joined antisocial activities like theft, robbery etc. Not only that, different persons used to utilize their acquired wealth in different manner, some persons used to enlarge their dwelling houses, some other used to take pride and pleasure in rearing large number of wild animals, yet others used to spend their fortune in collecting articles made of precious metals. There arose idea of private property, that also because of increase in number of artificial articles when there happened division of profession. Barter system or system of exchange of materials was in vogue in human society as long as number of articles did not increase significantly. It became difficult to collect articles in exchange of other articles when number of such articles increased to a great extent. Both parties had to carry materials for exchange at certain common place every time whenever any transaction used to take place. Not only that every time medium of exchange used to be different, but also it was difficult to determine value of materials or ratio of exchange. It aroused many long drawn bargaining and arguments. When potter used to join with a smith for exchange then medium of exchange were earthen pitchers bowls and cauldrons on the one hand and metallic daggers hoes axe etc. on the other. When that same potter became eager to exchange with a carpenter, mediums of exchange were earthen utensils and wooden furniture. Many persons expected certain common medium of exchange which was light for conveyance, easy to count and could be utilized to transact all kinds of articles and was equally acceptable to all to eliminate this trouble in determining medium of exchange. Initially certain popular food grain like rice or wheat, which was used equally by all, was determined as common medium of exchange. Food grains continued as common medium of exchange for a long time. But trouble of carrying medium of exchange was not thoroughly erased, large quantity of rice or wheat used to be carried during every exchange. Everyone expected certain medium small in size and light in weight for ease of carriage. Now shell was determined as medium. By that time system of administration appeared among mankind. Division of profession happened and Idea of private property became accepted social custom wherever large numbers of artificial articles were invented and circulated. Many persons became successful in their profession of production and distribution of articles, but many others were unsuccessful though were equally eager to consume and enjoy articles. They took resort to many antisocial activities like theft robbery etc. mankind felt need to institute administration to protect earned and private wealth of people living in society. Some people used to be ready with arms as guard round the clock as there was no particular time for committing crimes by such people involved in antisocial activities. Bands of people were appointed as sentinels at every human society, where large numbers of artificial articles were invented, to protect private property of people and one or few persons used to be appointed as leaders under whose command band of guards used to remain busy in protecting private property. System of administration was not created and introduced just for protecting private property from antisocial, many disputes and quarrels used to take place in relation to private property when idea of private property appeared on account of large number of articles. Disputes used to take place for settling area of land for dwelling places or land for cultivation, ensuring right of any person in his earned wealth and denying other persons from enjoying that wealth and various other grounds. Subsequently many other varieties of disputes, like taking loans and not repaying, purchasing articles on loan and not paying price etc arose when first shells and then metal coins were introduced as medium of exchange. We find similar disputes in these days among human beings. Disputes among mankind did not arise just on division of profession on account of increase in number of articles when idea of private property appeared. All men were successfully engaged in their professions till the time well after division of profession. Condition was not conducive to institute administration among mankind till that time. Also patriarchal order appeared in human society simultaneously with division of profession, but that was a custom in vogue in its primary stage and loosely followed. Articles were not sufficiently large in number and jobs in professions were not absolutely difficult to accomplish, as every producer was required to produce a very limited quantity of articles which could be sufficient to collect other articles produced by other producers, though jobs were done with physical labour, so women had participation in jobs. Women used to join in jobs in the past to produce articles along with others when number of articles was few. Lighter parts of jobs used to be performed by women and heavier parts used to be set aside to be performed by men though all jobs in those days were physically laborious. Women were not absolutely unemployed, hopelessly helpless and without support as they had some kind of participation in production of articles; patriarchy was not firmly established. All parts of any job, light or heavy, were required to be performed by persons selecting the job when division of profession appeared as a result of increase in number of articles and patriarchy became dominant social order. A woman would be required to perform all jobs of any profession would she select such a profession after division of profession. It was not possible for any woman in those days of all pervading physical strength, when all jobs were performed by application of physical strength, to select and perform all jobs of any profession with her individual capacity; they were unable to take part in economic activities and were thoroughly dependant on men for monetary reason and patriarchy arose. This patriarchal order was not firmly aground in society at initial stage of division of profession and rise of idea of private property as a result of increase in number of articles. Number of articles was not very large initially, it was little more above threshold to propel men to divide among professions, instead of producing conjointly. All members of any community used to produce all articles conjointly as long as number of such articles remained within a limit. Thereafter, in initial stage of division of profession, every producer was required to produce limited volume of materials which could be sufficient to allow him to collect all other required materials, as number of such materials for consumption was few or not very large till that time. Jobs in any profession were not huge to be painfully heavy. India during vedic period and subsequent Buddhist period provides us with certain evidences to draw conclusion about what happens to any civilised society which experiences division of profession as a result of increase in number of articles more than the threshold to propel all men to divide among professions, but such number remains stagnant or near stagnant and does not increase significantly for a continuous run of certain lengthy period by denying common people to get higher level education. India during that period did not produce large evidence of advancement in material civilisation, and added to that population in India was fewer, India was largely full of jungles with very few principal cities, but population there was not greatly huge. We can believe that jobs in professions were light during that period and women had participation in jobs for which patriarchy was not a strong social order and population did not increase. Works in professions were light because very few numbers of articles of consumption was in circulation, though division of profession happened. Every producer was required to produce limited volume of articles in his own profession to be able to collect other articles produced by other producers. Even women could take part in such production process in certain capacities when works were light, and patriarchy did not become firmly aground, and population did not increase. India during that lengthy period provides the example when there was few numbers of articles of consumption and low population, though there happened division of profession. Indian civilisation during Vedic and subsequent Buddhist period did not progress materially as a low standard of education was circulated among common people who could be possible inventors and producers of articles during that period, but who could not invent many articles as they were deprived to get higher education. Other civilisations progressed materially as higher standard of education was allowed for common people and large numbers of articles were invented. Everybody there felt eagerness to collect varieties of articles. Each producer there was required to produce articles in his profession in larger quantity so that he could collect many other articles. So jobs in each profession became heavier on account of increase in number of articles, and women were unable to join any profession when patriarchal order became dominant. Evidence of progress of material civilisation after Harappa Mohenjo-Daro civilisation is absent or not present in large volume in India during ancient age before Muslim occupation. Material civilisation did not progress in this region before initiation of Buddhism or during Brahmin period as education was strictly restricted among Brahmins, and non Brahmins were not entitled to get education. Division of profession arose in society with number of articles slightly more than number to allow people to work conjointly instead of dividing among profession, but patriarchy was at its initial stage and not very firmly established. Each producer used to produce a limited and low volume of articles which could be sufficient to enable him to collect all other articles of consumption in sufficient quantity. Work in each profession was light and even women could join such professions. Women did not become absolutely hopelessly helpless. Some parts of total jobs used to be accomplished by women, and domination by men folk over women could not be firmly established. Patriarchy was not firmly aground and population increase did not happen. While all other civilisations advanced materially for which works in professions became heavy to disallow women to join work, and they saw increase in population, India before Muslim domination did not advance materially and was free from harshly dominant patriarchy, as works in workshops were light which allowed women to participate in jobs, and population here did not increase. Difference in acquired wealth did not appear just on division of profession and initiation of material civilisation. All persons were still successful in their profession or in production and distribution of artificial articles and difference in wealth of persons was not yet that glaring though division of profession happened as a result of increase in number of articles at the initiation of division of profession. Disputes relating to personal properties were few in number during this initial stage of division of profession. Thereafter men continued inventing new articles and number of artificial articles continued to increase in civilisations outside India. Number of articles became so large at certain point of time that such jobs no longer remained light, rather those became heavy as any producer whoever used to intend to procure many other articles was required to produce large volume of articles for which works in profession became heavy and women became unable to participate production, patriarchy appeared and population started increasing very fast. Number of disputes relating to personal property increased with increase in population as pressure of population on limited volume of wealth increased. Requirement to introduce administration was felt more with increase in population. Division of profession arose already among mankind and as a result mankind was induced to join business or transaction and certain common acceptable food article was in circulation as medium of exchange. Legal tender money was not yet in circulation; money was introduced as medium of exchange after institution of administration when certain mark of administrator was impressed on certain thing to approve it as legal tender money. Many people were unsuccessful in their profession of production and distribution of articles and joined workshops belonging to others with fixed remuneration which made owners of such workshops wealthier, and difference between acquired wealth of many persons became visibly large when patriarchy appeared and population increased at faster rate. Those who were unsuccessful in their own profession, joined professions belonging to others as workers with fixed remuneration. Relation and difference of owner employee arose and members belonging to higher strata felt need to keep distance with people belonging to lower strata, and they felt need to cover themselves with clothes to add weight to their position. So mankind felt urge to be civilized when patriarchal order became dominant social custom on account of large scale increase of artificial consumable articles, population increased and many people were unsuccessful in their profession for which difference in acquired wealth arose in society as there existed rich and poor; and owners wanted to keep distance with employees. Mankind did not feel urge to be civilized just when knowledge was revealed among them. Man was still in primitive condition and did not become civilized though knowledge was revealed among mankind and education was circulated among ordinary people before material civilisation progressed to some length. That means mankind could develop knowledge to some extent even when it was in primitive condition. Therefore urge to be civilized does not germinate with exposure and development of knowledge. We find naked ascetics in India living in high altitude of the Himalayas and busy in acquiring highest order of knowledge who do not feel any urge to be civilized. Disputes arose in society relating to private property after idea of private property arose in mankind. Need for establishment of administration was felt to settle such social disputes and to protect men and their acquired private property from antisocial elements. Mankind felt need to be civilized to cover themselves with clothes to maintain distance between rulers and ruled, managers and subordinates, rich and poor. But man did not feel, for the first time, need to cover themselves with clothes to be civilized only when this need was felt by rulers; even before that it was felt to establish administration when many persons were unsuccessful in their profession on rise of division of profession and idea of private property as a result of increase of artificial articles, and many of them joined professions belonging to others as workers with fixed remuneration; and employer employee relation came into existence. Difference in acquired wealth arose in society and persons possessing larger wealth and owners wanted to keep distance with workers and less wealthy and felt need to be civilized. Mankind felt need to cover themselves with clothes to be civilized as a result of difference of wealth when persons holding larger and lower wealth and owners and employees were created.

Education was definitely circulated among ordinary people in those areas where invention of articles advanced among mankind. Ordinary people were entitled to get education in all centers of civilisation like Harappa Mohenjo-Daro Sumer Mesopotamia Assyria Egypt etc. Progress of material civilisation is proof for that. But evidences are there that knowledge was exposed among human beings in some areas other than these centers of civilisation. All those Harappa Mohenjo-Daro Lothal etc are evidences of ancient civilisation in India. That civilisation existed at least five thousand years ago and it ended suddenly at least around 1500 years ago before Christ without keeping any legacy. Material evidences whatever is found next to extensive evidences of ancient Harappan civilisation on Indian soil are Buddhist monasteries. Those were built after 500 BC, after appearance of Lord Buddha, definitely not before that. There was a void of at least 1000 years in between end of Harappan civilisation and rise of Buddhist civilisation. That was the period which is known as Vedic or Brahmin period (both are synonymous). No one knows with certainty what happened on Indian soil during that void. We do not find material evidences of any king kingdom city or town of that era. Only evidences of that era which are available are Vedas, Brahmins, Upanishads, Ramayana, Mahabharata, Kalidas, Panini etc. There was a section in society called Brahmin. Members of this section were thoroughly engaged in exercise of acquisition of knowledge and never joined production and distribution of articles. Group of people in India who were engaged with production and distribution of articles were not entitled to get education better than very basic level. They could invent and produce few numbers of articles, which were one step better than articles produced with basic elementary instincts and intuitions, utilizing that very basic education. Material civilisation did not make much headway and remained standstill there in India with the help of that most elementary education circulated among people who could be actual inventors and producers of artificial articles in those days would they get higher education. They were engaged for generations in most primary divisions of professions like cultivation, husbandry, carpentry, masonry etc getting that elementary level of education. Such absence of articles also proves that Brahmins in India who were always engaged to acquire knowledge never invented and produced any article. There was division of profession and idea of private property arose in Indian society and these customs were in vogue in their most primary form. Simultaneously certain administrative machinery was there in most primary stage. It is difficult to guess whether there was any king queen kingdom during Brahmin era though Puranas, which are considered as ancient Indian history of Brahmin or Vedic era compiled in loose manner, not following universal rules of writing history remaining unbiased and true to facts only, and where facts legends fables gods goddesses myths truths were all intermingled and from where it is extremely difficult to extract truths, contain few mentions of kings. Was there any group of people during Vedic era between Brahmins and non Brahmin producers in India? What was their position in society, were they engaged with administrative machinery of that time? What kind of administration did exist during that period? Would we find existence of any group of people, who were entitled to education, in India during Vedic period between educated Brahmins and ill educated non Brahmin producers, it will be another mystery of ancient India which was not unfolded. We can guess that this assumed group of people, whose existence was uncertain, between Brahmins and non Brahmin producers were allowed to join education but they would not join education with any commitment to reach highest level of knowledge as they were non Brahmins. Would there exist in reality any group of people in India during Vedic period who were non Brahmins but were allowed to get education, then why did material civilisation not progress on Indian soil during that period? Where were centers of administration if such non Brahmin educated people during that period were engaged with administration? We know legendary works by some Indians during ancient period which are considered as timeless and invaluable contributions in different branches of knowledge like those of Kalidas Varbi and others in literature, medical books by Charak and Shushruta, astronomical and mathematical books by Barahamihir, Aryabhatta and others, economics by Chanakya etc. Some branches of knowledge found their origin in India like grammar and economics which were not known to outside world for a long time. Many of those scholars who made valuable contributions might be non Brahmins. If some of those non Brahmin scholars, who made valuable contributions in fields of knowledge, appeared during Vedic period before Buddhism then naturally it can be concluded that non Brahmins were allowed to get education during that period. But then what were their professions? Were these all non Brahmins but educated engaged in administrative machinery only and not in production and distribution of articles? Articles of Brahmin period are not available. Also how many persons administrative machinery could accommodate? And if so many persons were engaged with administration only without joining any other profession then administrative machineries in those days in Brahmin period were strong and widespread, but where were those centers of administration? We did not get satisfactory answers to all such disturbing questions. We can be slightly relieved of all these questions if it is accepted that these scholars appeared in Buddhist period only after end of Brahmin era, as a larger section of people were allowed to get education after initiation of Buddhism, as evidences of higher order of articles in larger volume and centers of power of Buddhist era are extant. We have to remain calm and content in absence of evidence to conclude that there was no section of population, who were allowed to get education, between educated Brahmins and ill educated producers of articles during Brahmin period. Patriarchal order was not firmly aground in India in absence of large number of articles as common people were allowed to get only most primary education. Population in India did not increase agonizingly during that period in absence of dominant patriarchy and most of the land was covered with jungles where there used to live primitive people. They never felt need to be civilized, being devoid of right to get education, as they could not invent and circulate large number of articles. Brahmins used to join exercise of knowledge with commitment to reach highest order of knowledge and they were forbidden to divert their attention to anything else ending their exercise at certain intermediate stage. Absence of progress of material civilisation is a kind of proof that right of education was strictly restricted in the hands of Brahmins in India before spread of Buddhism, and non Brahmins were not entitled to get education. Artificial articles were invented by non Brahmins ending their education at certain intermediate stage everywhere on earth wherever they were allowed to get education, and artificial articles were invented produced and circulated in the hands of such persons. Brahmins did not invent articles of consumption. Mankind produced few primary articles with the help of elementary basic instincts and intuitions, which qualities were congenital within everybody and need not be learnt – blunt stone made weapons, huts made of branches and leaves, bows and arrows, spears, axe etc. Probably men at different places independently invented and developed such primary articles as no extra acquired knowledge better than elementary instincts and intuitions were required for making such articles. Probably such articles were not invented at certain particular places on earth from where these were circulated everywhere else. We notice use of such articles among people everywhere – even among people living in far off islands or dense jungles who have no contact with civilized people outside. Where from did they learn production processes of such articles? And how have they been producing such articles for generations after inventing these articles as they have no touch with education? Only reason how they have been able to produce such articles for generations with unbroken continuity is that such articles do not require any extra acquired knowledge higher than elementary instincts and intuitions and people everywhere are endowed naturally with same level of basic instincts. Certain extra acquired knowledge particularly those of number system and system of measurement were required for Invention and production of next stage articles such as carts with wheels, building brick made houses, wooden doors and windows, furniture, wooden or metal boxes etc. Here difference was made at this stage between circulation of extra acquired knowledge and non circulation. Non Brahmin ordinary people were able to invent and produce next stage advanced articles wherever they were allowed to get education. Such ordinary people failed to invent advanced articles where they did not earn right to get education. They remained and even now remain confined among those primary articles which can be invented and produced utilizing elementary instincts and intuitions. All groups of primitive people, who are living still at different corners on earth, such as those in Medak and Malkangiri districts of Orissa and Bastar district in Madhya Pradesh in India, few red Indian tribes in Amazon jungle in south America, some such tribes living scattered here and there in Africa, aborigines living in Darwin state in Australia, people in far away Polynesian islands are all remaining confined in few primary articles and did not advance further. No knowledge has ever been circulated among such people as these peoples never discovered any knowledge nor did they acquire knowledge from outside as they have no contact with outside world. But we cannot assume that knowledge was never revealed among primitive people everywhere wherever such people exist. Now primitive people are restricted to move within certain small areas in India, as civilised people increased in number and occupied most of the lands, but once upon a time entire land belonged to them. Entire country east of desert of Rajasthan and Gujarat was covered with jungle. Of course population was also low at that time. Primitive people used to live in jungle, but there were many localities inhabited by civilized people, among whom were Brahmins and non Brahmin producers of articles who were allowed very basic elementary level of education and used to earn livelihood for generations joining few primary professions. Such producers could not progress very far in invention and production of artificial articles. Brahmins were thoroughly engaged in study of Vedas Upanishads etc. knowledge and education were not circulated among all people though such knowledge was revealed among some section of people in the same country and though such civilized Brahmins and primitive people used to live at that time in close proximity. Today primitive people in India are confined in few small areas and for which there is large distance between their habitats and those of other sections of population, but distance was not so large between primitive people and other sections of population in India 2500 years ago or even before during Brahmin period when entire land was covered with jungle and primitive people used to live all over the land. They used to live practically within visible range of Brahmins who had access to knowledge. But such primitive people were never allowed opportunity to join education. Everywhere else in the world, wherever civilisation has progressed, people used to live in primitive condition in the past; but they were allowed to join education even when they were primitive after knowledge was revealed among them, and they became civilized. But this cycle of events did not happen in India.

Buddhist monasteries were evidences of artificial articles in India after Harappa Mohenjo-Daro civilisation. No evidence of production and distribution of articles is available in India during long intermediate period of void. But there were Vedas Upanishads Ramayana Mahabharata etc. That means knowledge was exposed among some section of people long ego but it was not circulated among all. Primitive people in India produced primary stage articles long ago during ancient time utilizing basic intuitions, but there power to invent ended there. They failed to invent and produce newer varieties of artificial articles. We do not find evidence of artificial articles in India during Brahmin period. Brahmins never joined in invention and production of articles, and non Brahmins were unable to invent articles because they were not allowed to join education.

Aztec and Maya civilisations were spread in Mexico Guatemala Honduras and other countries which are in southern part of North America. Inca civilisation was spread in Peru Columbia Venezuela in north western part of South America. Many cities and town are still extant in this vast land as evidences of those lost civilisations. Now most of these ancient cities and towns are deserted but once during the time when such civilisations were in full glory, those were inhabited by large number of people. These ancient cities and towns were full of people during invasion of the Spanish. All features of material civilisation were distinctly and prominently present in such habitats. Common people earned right to get education, large number of articles of consumption were invented and circulated in society. But that was a period of all pervading physical strength, mechanization of job was a far cry during that time, women were incapable to join any economic job of production of articles on account of physically laborious nature of production process, and became thoroughly dependent on men as they became confined to remain behind wall. Patriarchal system appeared in society and population increased rapidly. Division of profession, idea of private property and business appeared as a result of invention and circulation of large number of articles. Thereafter dominant patriarchal order or unquestioned and unconditional authority of men on women came into force and population started to increase at a very fast rate when numbers of articles were so large that each producer had to produce large volume of articles and jobs in professions became heavy so that women became thoroughly incapable to join any profession. Everyone was required to select his own profession for division of profession. But many persons were unsuccessful in their profession of production and distribution of articles and joined professions of other persons as workers with fixed remuneration. Difference in acquired wealth of persons appeared and high and low status of people arose in society, even slave system was found among Maya Inca Aztec people. All possible features of material civilisation were present among them. Primitive people, among whom there was no circulation of education, and invention and production of articles were impossible, used to live in small groups scattered and well away from each other in land covered with dense jungle outside civilized areas of both of Americas. Material civilisation did not progress among primitive people, their effort to produce articles was restricted within few primary articles, which were in vogue during ancient time, and which men could produce utilizing their basic instincts and intuitions. Probably civilisations in both of Americas are not very ancient and they started around 1500 to 2000 years ago from now, ordinary people were allowed to join education from around this time and articles were invented and circulated. These civilisations were gradually spreading in all directions to capture surrounding jungles, population was increasing among civilized nations, lands used to be recovered and localities were founded and spread by eliminating jungles to accommodate increased population and grow food for them. Probably these civilisations would pervade entire continents would time permit them. But the Spanish captured and destroyed civilized areas of both of Americas before that could happen, and for this reason vast lands in both of Americas were full of jungles where civilisation did not spread during Spanish invasion.

Africa had its civilized areas in north of the continent, in Egypt and Carthez (now Tunisia). Material civilisation advanced to a great extent in such centers, large number of articles were invented and circulated and population increased. But rest of the continent outside these two centers of civilisation, particularly vast land south of Sahara was filled with dense jungle and water bodies, inhabited by wild animals, where no civilisation ever initiated and progressed, and primitive people used to live, among whom population did not increase. Knowledge did not reveal among natives of Australia and Polynesian islands, material civilisation did not advance there and population did not increase. Civilisation spread far and wide to cover vast lands in Asia and Europe and both of Americas, except in India, which means civilized people spread and covered vast lands in these continents. Knowledge revealed among certain groups of people in some centers of these continents during ancient time and common people were allowed to join education. They invented and circulated many artificial articles of consumption, material civilisation arose among them and population increased as a result. Either increased population among civilized nations in those days spread and covered vast lands in those continents, or primitive people in those days living far and near who did not see light of civilisation till that time were inspired seeing progress of civilisation in such centers of civilisation to join civilisation, and invited and allowed all people of their communities to join education and production of articles. It is not precisely known when primitive people vanished from Europe and Asia except India and some parts of South East Asia. We only know that the Greeks did not invade north and west Europe, which can indicate that peoples living in those lands did not advance significantly materially during dominance of the Greeks. But Romans invaded and occupied those lands. Peoples there advanced significantly in material civilisation by that time to attract Romans. In Asia also we find civilised people spread and occupied all lands except India and South East Asia. Probably increased people from few centers of civilisation in these two continents, where knowledge was revealed and who saw light of civilisation first before others, as circulation of education among ordinary people was acknowledged among them which led them to invent large number of articles, did not spread in surrounding lands eliminating and annihilating or just swallowing and erasing separating identity of natives of those lands, who till that time did not become civilized, as otherwise languages of centers of civilisation, where people became more wealthy and powerful, as they saw rise of civilisation or production of articles, would spread and become dominant languages in surrounding lands removing primitive people. But so many living nations and their languages in Europe and Asia is sufficient proof that languages of certain centers of civilisation did not spread to become dominant everywhere. All these linguistic groups did not experience rise of civilisation at the same time, and many of them were vanquished and subjugated by others. But even then no single or few languages became dominant in these two continents. We have to always keep into consideration that no civilized nation ever conducted military expedition against any primitive uncivilized nation, who were totally devoid of any knowledge to create wealth, as there was no possibility of plundering wealth by invading primitive people. Civilized nations never conducted military expedition in areas inhabited by primitive people to uproot and drive away them to recover land and settle increased population. Then how did primitive people join civilisation? How did peoples at different places maintain their separate linguistic identity? One possible reason may be that primitive people, living in surrounding areas contiguous to any center of civilisation, where knowledge was exposed and common people were allowed to get education and many articles were produced, were inspired to join civilisation inviting all members of their communities to join education and production. Once they progressed to reach certain level of civilisation when they accumulated sufficient wealth to attract attention of civilized nation, which joined civilisation earlier and became a dominant force by that time, they were invaded and subjugated by civilized nation. The nation which was in primitive condition till later time and which joined civilisation later came to learn advanced knowledge coming into contact of civilized nation and learnt production of advanced articles in their subjugated condition. After some time such subjugated nations progressed to a significant extent in material civilisation to acquire strength to repulse victorious dominant nation and established themselves as a strong and independent linguistic group. Asia Minor and surrounding areas were under control of Greeks when they were a dominant force. It is not easy to say whether people living in and around Asia Minor and surrounding areas became civilized coming into contact with Greeks or even before when they came into contact with Egyptians and Sumerians. Human history is not written in such detailed fashion till now so that we can get answers to all questions. Similarly northern and western Europe except Scandinavia and west Asia came under control of Rome. Western and northern European nations were uncivilized and did not join accumulation of wealth to attract attention of Greeks when Greeks were a dominant force. But during Roman dominance they achieved significant progress in material civilisation, though far low in level of progress than Rome and equally less powerful, and Rome was tempted to grab their lands and wealth. These subjugated nations in captured lands, who were till that time lower in civilisation and among whom certain lower level of education was in circulation and were backward in producing artificial articles, became eager to attain level of civilisation reached by Rome when they came into contact of Rome during period of subjugation. Now they circulated higher level education among members of their communities and started producing higher level articles. European nations like German French Spanish English were inferior in civilisation during Roman dominance but rapidly achieved level of civilisation attained by Romans and started producing advanced articles as they learnt advanced knowledge under subjugation. Civilisation might not be introduced among Europeans by Romans but they progressed rapidly and many steps of civilisation under Roman subjugation. Some of those subjugated nations in Europe became significantly strong and finally dominant in production and business of articles as they accumulated large fortune in the process, when progress of civilisation became rapid under subjugation, and finally they achieved liberty. The Germans became such a formidable power that after few centuries in early part of sixth century they vanquished and subjugated the Romans from whom they were inspired to be civilized, from which subjugation the Romans were never liberated and at certain time around 820-21 AD the Western Roman empire became Holy Roman Empire of Germanic Tribes. The empire was Roman only by name but was actually ruled by Germans and center of power was in France and Germany from where Charlemagne and posterity ruled. Did central Asian nations take part in same turn of events? The Turks Tajiks Kazaks and other nations maintained their identity as separate linguistic groups. If civilisation did not initiate independently among them, then did they earn spirit of civilisation from Sumer or later day Parsees under whom they were subjugated, and at certain point of time these subjugated nations attained strength to drive away victorious nations to maintain their independent identity?

Description of progress of material civilisation of nations is not included in present style of writing history. But artificial articles of consumption are at the root of initiation of material civilisation and its progress. Division of profession, idea of private property arose in mankind, business or transaction became principal activity among mankind, system of administration was introduced and money was circulated as a result of production of artificial articles and increase in their number. But description of progress in the field of invention production and distribution of articles is not included in study of history as this idea is not clearly known to humankind. Description of invention of article by any particular human group and wealth accumulated in the process of doing business in that article is not found in books of history. We can find only description of rise of certain nations in certain areas and invasion by one nation of other nations. But the knowledge that artificial articles were at the root of rise of any human group and even now all activities of business and commerce among mankind are progressing continuously circling around invention and distribution of artificial articles is not clearly known. Artificial articles are at the root why human group of a certain area attacks other human groups. Jobs in professions become heavy as a result of increase in number of articles, and all jobs in the past were dependant on physical strength. Women were unable to join any physically strenuous and heavy job, they became helpless without any monetary support as they had no participation in economic job to earn, and became thoroughly dependant on men. Women lost all right on property and patriarchy became dominant social order. Idea of private property became social practice and idea of profit and loss in business was accepted on account of increase in number of articles. Some people, who were successful in business, earned and accumulated huge wealth and at certain time society decided that men's own children would inherit their earned wealth. Shame was imposed on women and they were confined behind wall. But men folk forgot reason why women were confined behind door once they were so confined. Men folk started feeling unreasonable curiosity about women. Population started increasing rapidly as a result of helpless dependence of women on men on the one hand and curiosity of men about women on the other. Increase in number of articles creates situation for patriarchal dominance which is at the root of increase in population. Population increased in those areas on earth where in the past common people were allowed to join education, articles were invented and developed and material civilisation arose. Deficiency in produced articles happened among mankind as a result of increase in population. Many people became rich as many of them became poor as a result of division of profession and business. Volume of articles produced was not sufficient to meet demand of people of country and price of deficient articles increased irrationally which resulted in increase in incidences of theft robbery and other antisocial activities. A large number of people, mostly drawn from poor section of population, used to be united under umbrella of military force to attack some other country to get relief from such problems. Intention used to be plundering. Some such country used to be selected for invasion where civilisation has appeared and wealth accumulation has been initiated and continued for some time so that large booty could be acquired by invading. Such countries or lands were never attacked where civilisation did not appear and collection and accumulation of wealth was not initiated, and possibility was bleak to be richer by attacking and subjugating them. Do we find anywhere in books of history that Egypt and in later day Greece and Rome conducted military expeditions in Africa south of Sahara where civilisation was never initiated and no wealth was accumulated and there was no possibility of plundering rich booty by attacking such land? The Egyptian pharaohs used to conduct military expeditions in west Asia and Mesopotamia where people were civilized and wealth was accumulated. Never had they conducted such expedition next to their home in Africa which was covered with jungle. The Greek warlord Alexander eyed only civilized areas on earth where wealth was accumulated when he led his expedition before 333 BC. Asia Minor Persia western India and Egypt were victims of his attacks. Last pharaoh of Egypt accepted Alexander's supremacy without waging war. West Europe did not attract attention of Alexander, that means though civilisation started in some centers in west Europe and education was circulated among ordinary people, that was in its primary stage when large variety of articles was not produced, and sufficient wealth to attract attention was not accumulated among nations in west Europe. But why Rome could not attract attention of Alexander? Was it because Rome did not progress sufficiently to accumulate sufficient wealth to attract attention during Alexander? But administration was introduced in Rome at around 753 BC, which indicates that artificial articles were invented and circulated in Rome before that, people there were aware of idea of private property. Even Rome introduced some kind of administration similar to democracy following footsteps of Athens when elderly members of communities used to be elected to join senate where they used to elect 2 consuls every year who were similar to dictators or elected rulers of Greece. Rome started creating and collecting wealth long before Alexander and it continued during Alexander. Introduction of administration was sufficient proof that people In Rome learnt about wealth and were creating wealth, there happened to be many disputes among people, thefts robberies and other antisocial activities as a result of wealth, if they had already learnt about many artificial articles by that time, and patriarchy appeared when population increased for production of large number of articles as works in professions became heavy, and many people failed in their professions to join antisocial activities. People in Rome felt need to institute administration to settle such dispute relating to property and to protect private property from thieves and robbers. But we are unable to learn extent of wealth accumulated in Rome during Alexander. Why Rome failed to attract attention of Alexander, or did the senate of Rome send large presentation of precious materials to Alexander to save Rome from his fury? Only historians can throw light. Civilisations in west Europe did not progress very far, and large volume of wealth was not created and accumulated there during dominance of Greece. But volumes of wealth to attract attention was created and accumulated in some centers of west Europe during dominance of Rome which attracted attention of Rome. Rome captured one by one all countries in west and north Europe, France, England, Germany, Spain except Scandinavia. Civilisation initiated in such countries, education was circulated among common people and they invented many artificial articles. Wealth was created and accumulated among them. But they were far behind Rome of that time in respect of invention and production of artificial articles though civilisation was initiated and in was force for certain length of time among them. Lower level of education, compared to level of education in circulation among Romans, was in circulation among people of these countries, and they could produce articles of lower order and joined business with such articles. These countries were recent participants in civilisation. They were less advanced than Rome in developing weapons and were weaker militarily. Their military forces were no match for Rome's military. They became vanquished and subjugated under

Rome. These subjugated nations in captured lands, who were far backward compared to Romans In respect of attainment of level of civilisation, now acquired advanced education after coming into contact with Romans during subjugation and learnt to produce many advanced articles. They could now produce advanced war machines and built formidable military forces. Civilisation might not be initiated among European primitive people when they came into contact with Romans – they saw light of civilisation few centuries ago – it progressed many steps under subjugation. Some of these nations acquired profuse strength in production and business of articles and formed strong military force. The Germans became so strong that after few centuries in first quarter of sixth century the Ostrogoths vanquished and subjugated the Romans from whom they learnt production of many articles, from which subjugation the Romans could never free themselves, and in first quarter of ninth century around 820-21 the western Roman empire was declared as Holy Roman Empire of Germanic Tribes. It was Roman Empire only by name, it was ruled actually by Germans. Subjugated nations maintained their independent identity as separate linguistic groups learning advanced knowledge and production processes of articles from victors to be strong when they repulsed victors. Did central Asian nations take part in same turns of events? The Turks Tajiks Kazaks and other nations have been maintaining their separate identity as linguistic groups. Did they become subjugated to Sumer or later day Parsees from whom they learnt elements of civilisation, if civilisation did not initiate independently among them, and drove away victors after acquiring strength to maintain independent identity? This trend of material civilisation is in force even now. Nations which are unsuccessful in inventing new articles are unable to join in business of such articles, workshops or production units are not built in their countries to produce such articles though people of such countries show eagerness to consume and enjoy such articles, for which such articles are imported from other countries which have attained success in inventing and producing such articles, less amount of taxes and duties relating to production and sale is deposited in government's coffer of unsuccessful countries and they remain poor, while exporting countries become richer. In the past backward and poor countries used to be invaded and captured by some other stronger country. Now a days it is not possible to maintain such aggressive attitude. Now the countries which are unsuccessful in business of articles invite engineers and businessmen from countries who have achieved success in invention and production of articles to build arrangements (factories) for production and distribution of article in unsuccessful countries. In return businessmen from successful countries take in his country part of profits earned in business done in unsuccessful countries. Thereafter people of unsuccessful countries may sometimes be inspired, if they feel urge to arouse their genuine intention, learn production processes of articles to join production from businessmen and engineers of successful countries whom they have invited to set up industries in unsuccessful countries. But artificial articles of consumption are at the root of all such turns of events.

Common people paid attention in invention of articles in those centers where such people were allowed to join education, but who joined exercise of education without commitment to attain ultimate level of knowledge, unlike Brahmins in India, and ended education at certain intermediate stages, and all articles were invented in the hands of such people. Can we presume that mankind became acquainted with certain new knowledge simultaneously with invention of new articles, which indicates that mankind did not know of certain knowledge before invention? It is true that a new invention of something, be it certain idea or article, is a new addition to store of knowledge which was not known to mankind earlier. Mankind comes to learn about certain new knowledge only when it is discovered or invented, before that it is unknown. All those new discoveries in different branches are new knowledge to mankind. Volumes of different branches inflated as new facts and truths were discovered and knowledge of mankind also increased in same proportion. Then how is it proved that mankind knew something before discovery of facts in branches of knowledge or mankind did not come to know certain knowledge simultaneously with discovery of facts and those branches of knowledge were already known even before discovery? But we also noticed that knowledge was already exposed in India but did not find exhibition in artificial articles as common people were deprived to join education. Coming to this stage we have to slightly modify our idea. There is one particular branch of knowledge at the root of advancement of knowledge and material civilisation, that is knowledge of number system. One earns right to join a branch of science when one is acquainted with knowledge of number system. Knowledge of number system is at the root of exercise in any branch of science and material civilisation, branch of science is developed depending on knowledge of number system. Material civilisation advanced in areas where number system exposed. Also system of measurement was invented utilizing knowledge of number. That number system might not be higher mathematics but was at least primary mathematics or arithmetic. Number system found exposure long ago, many millenniums ago. The Ishango bone in central Africa was as old as 18000 to 20000 BC. The Lebombo bones of Swaziland are even older, almost 35000 years ago BC. Many people think that such arrangements of bones indicate certain mathematical idea, though this claim is disputed. Evidences of this knowledge of mankind in prehistoric time have been found at different places like England (other than Stonehenge), Scotland,

France etc. probably people at different places independently came to learn about number system. Probably number system was not discovered by any particular group of persons at certain particular place from where this knowledge was propagated everywhere. Number system might be exposed even among human groups living in far off islands and dense jungles which are inaccessible and without communication with civilized world. It is commonly believed that number system might have been revealed for certain practical purpose, like counting of cattle, building houses, measuring cultivable land or for counting days, months and years. But population did not increase painfully before rise of civilization when number of articles was vary few and division of profession and patriarchy did not appear. There was plenty of cultivable land as compared to number of population, if artificial cultivation would already be invented, and probably many people would cultivate same land to distribute products of land equally among themselves. It can be concluded with certainty that number system was not discovered for measuring private lands or for settling disputes relating to land if number system was already known at a time when there was no idea of private property in the absence of large number of articles. Division of profession cannot arise depending on just one profession, artificial cultivation, and it does not create awareness of idea of private property. Many people of community can join that profession unitedly, they can cultivate any piece of land which does not belong to any particular person. Division of profession arises with large number of articles when nobody can perform all jobs, and it creates idea of private property. Not only that, women fail to join jobs on account of physically strenuous nature of jobs when patriarchy becomes dominant and population increases. But cultivable land at any place cannot be stretched to any length and breath to satisfy demand of land by increased population, and disputes appear as pressure of population on land increases with increase of population. Only then it is required to measure land to determine private lands of persons and to settle disputes relating to land. Number system was required to measure land when division of profession already arose in society, mankind became aware of idea of private property, many articles were invented and produced, works in workshops became heavy when women became unable to join profession and many disputes arose relating to land as a result of pressure of increase population on land. But long before that division of profession appeared among mankind and they became aware of idea of private property for circulation of large number of articles, and that was possible by inventing measurement system utilizing number system. Articles were invented and increased in number everywhere wherever system of measurement was invented using number system. So cultivable lands were required to be measured only when population increased and pressure of population on land was increased. Population increased as patriarchy became dominant social custom as jobs in those days were physically laborious for which women were unable to join jobs. Jobs became laborious for invention and circulation of large number of artificial articles when there appeared division of profession, and awareness of idea of private property was created among mankind as nobody was able to perform all jobs or produce all articles for increase in their number. A job does not remain physically strenuous when different parts of job are done by different persons and women also can join such jobs. But that same job becomes laborious when it is required to be performed by one person individually after division of profession. Division of profession arose among mankind for large number of articles and that number increased when system of measurement was invented using number system. Number system was not discovered for measuring agricultural lands. Mankind came to learn number system long and many steps before requirement to measure cultivable land to settle dispute created by population pressure. Mankind reached stage of requirement of measurement of agricultural land crossing many stages after acquaintance with number system. At best we can say that mankind utilized already known number system when in future he required to measure land to settle land related disputes which happened on account of population pressure for increased population. Mankind came to know number system long before building brick built houses, so number system did not arise for building houses. Brick built houses were created sometimes near initiation of civilisation, around 5000-6000 years ago, mankind knew about burnt bricks during that time. But mankind came to learn number system long before that. Number system was not discovered for the purpose of erecting houses. It is better to say that number system was utilized to invent many artificial articles including houses, or measuring cultivable land etc. Rest is astronomy, continuous passing by of days and nights, change of locations of sun moon and stars and other celestial bodies, which inspired men to learn number system. It can be concluded that number system was discovered for zeal of humankind to learn nature. Man discovered number in the process of study of nature. And this knowledge was there in store of mankind before initiation of civilisation or invention of articles.

So mankind came to learn about number system long before civilisation initiated. Can we imagine that the knowledge which men acquired during Vedic period in India did not have subject matter suitable for application in material civilisation for which we do not find evidence of civilisation in India during Vedic period? Either there was resource suitable for material civilisation in knowledge known to Indians during Vedic period which was not circulated among common Indians, common people were deprived of right of education, or there was no resource suitable for material civilisation in Indian knowledge for which no civilisation appeared on Indian soil during vedic period. The Vedic civilisation started after sudden destruction of Harappa Mohenjo-Daro and ended around 500 BC when Buddhism appeared. The city of Mohenjo-Daro was built according to geometric plan, roads were absolutely straight, and probably Mohenjo-Daro is world's earliest planned city. So men there came to know number system before that civilisation. Large numbers of artificial articles of that civilisation have been found, such articles could not be produced without creating system of measurement. So it is reasonable to think that number system with which Indians were acquainted from before Harappa Mohenjo-Daro civilisation was not altogether lost and found place in ancient books of Vedas Upanishads even after destruction of that civilisation. In reality we need not suppose, there are large numbers of instances of mathematics in Vedas. But ordinary non Brahmins were not allowed to know that mathematics and no measuring system was invented with that.

It is clear that mankind came to know about artificial articles only after being acquainted with knowledge of number system, or more specifically after inventing measuring system with that. But why should only non Brahmins be held responsible for inventing artificial articles? Human groups living in inaccessible lands far away from civilized world were not acquainted with number system for want of communication. So people living in inaccessible lands did not learn number and measurement system and were incapable to invent articles better than most primary articles. Material civilisation did not progress among them. But primitive human groups who lived in close proximity of and who had easy communication with civilized society could be aware of number. Everybody in any society does not utilize opportunity to get education though everybody has right of and equal access to it. Did large number of people remain ill educated voluntarily, and consequently remained primitive, following this nature, even while living in close proximity of civilized people, and though they had right to education similar to other sections of population? Material civilisation did not develop in India during Vedic period. Was it because ordinary non Brahmin people would like to keep distance voluntarily from system of education? And India during that time was full of jungles largely inhabited by primitive people, rather localities inhabited by civilised and educated people were few, so it was quite probable that many of such primitive groups of people resided very close to and within visible range of civilised people. Now a day we find primitive people living in small pockets well away from civilised people as most of the lands are captured and covered by civilised people, but once upon a time in distant past most of the lands were under control of primitive people. Even then they did not draw inspiration from civilised people to join education. And other non Brahmins who were actual producers of articles and living along with Brahmins were not entitled to get higher education which disabled them to invent and produce articles. Did such primitive people and non Brahmin people voluntarily and deliberately use to keep distance from education? But long before this during Harappa Mohenjo-Daro period ordinary people used to join education voluntarily without hesitation, as otherwise material civilisation or process of production of articles could not function and continue. Again they agreed to get a low level of education in later days during spread of Buddhism. Some articles higher in order than primary articles made during Buddhist period are available. Common people were deprived of right to get education though Vedas contained knowledge of mathematics. We are now unable to know whether Greece Rome west Asia independently became acquainted with number or learnt it from outside. We found evidences of number at different places on earth. Artificial articles were not invented till the time when such evidences came into being. Number system came to be known long before that. Similarly it was known among American red Indians many thousand years ago when they were still uncivilised. Brahmin religion or caste was not in force anywhere outside India. Division of Brahmin and non Brahmin was in vogue only in this India. So number system was exposed to certain casteless group of people if it became known independently at many places outside India. Also number system was exposed in India long before creation of Brahmins. Brahmin caste appeared after Harappa Mohenjo-Daro destruction according to historians though Brahmin caste and Sanatan (timeless) religion are much more ancient according to common belief. Beginning of Sanatan religion and Brahmin caste and their dominance is not known clearly to anybody according to common belief though there is no dispute regarding end of this dominance; the ancient Brahmin or Sanatan religion ended with rise of Buddhism. Nobody knows who is correct, whether Brahmin caste and Sanatan religion appeared long ago even before Harappa Mohenjo-Daro civilisation or these came into being only after destruction of that civilisation. We can conclude with certainty that number system came to be known in India before Vedic period or creation of Brahmin if opinion of historians is correct that Vedic period started after sudden destruction of Harappa Mohenjo-Daro civilisation, if we also suppose that Brahmins were created during Vedic period, there was no existence of Brahmins before that. So number system did not reveal in India among Brahmins, but subsequently they got complete possession on this branch of knowledge though they did not use that knowledge for any practical purpose. We fail to conclude whether number revealed itself to Brahmins or a casteless group of people in India if Vedas and Brahmins were created before Harappa Mohenjo-Daro according to popular belief. Brahmins can never claim credit of discovery and development of number system if it was exposed at different places outside India where there was no Brahmin non Brahmin division. Everyone in those casteless societies got right to learn that knowledge, it was not restricted in the hands of certain section of people. Many persons of those casteless societies who acquired that knowledge utilized it for production of artificial articles. But how far it is appropriate to say that artificial articles were created in the hands of non Brahmins in casteless societies where there was no division like Brahmin non Brahmin is arguable. Who was Brahmin and who was non Brahmin in a casteless society? All were equal there. To speak correctly members of all strata of such casteless society took part in creation of artificial articles, members of all strata were claimant of that credit. Brahmins used to follow a particular lifestyle only in this India where there was caste division like Brahmin non Brahmin, for which they never joined in creation and consumption of artificial articles, at least as long as the Brahmin period continued, and their whole hearted intention was to reach ultimate stage of knowledge. Only here artificial articles were created in the hands of non Brahmins. But why did Brahmin non Brahmin caste division appear only in India among all countries in the world? What was requirement to create a class called Brahmin? Was ultimate knowledge revealed in India written in Vedas Upanishads? Long ago in distant past there was a time full of bliss when mankind was still in primitive condition but they had fully matured and developed senses like man, but large numbers of articles were not yet found, as it was before knowledge of number, patriarchy did not appear and population did not increase. Pressure of population was still absent, population did not yet increase painfully and dense jungles were there surrounding their habitats where there were sufficient foods. Men did not use to toil hard to collect food. Artificial articles were low in number, and division of profession did not appear. All members of community used to collect and distribute food conjointly and equally. Men did not use to spend much time and energy for doing this much job. Mankind used to enjoy long leisurely time after finishing few numbers of jobs, whichever were there, spending limited amount of time and energy. What did men use to do during that long leisurely period? Did they use to participate in social and cultural activities? Probably some human groups in certain centers reached unanimous decision to join in discussion and deliberation about nature during this time while uniting in social and cultural activities to pass leisurely time. That was a time of peaceful comfort without much work when mankind advanced very far in the fields of knowledge. Did mankind come to know ultimate knowledge during this time? Then it is easily understandable and agreeable that ultimate knowledge was revealed among mankind before rise of civilisation. Mankind was still in primitive condition and large numbers of articles were not in circulation among them, division of profession did not rise and there was no awareness of idea of private property, wealth was not created among them, there was no difference of wealth. All were equal and men did not feel urge to be civilized. The Brahmins cannot claim credit for discovery development and progress of knowledge if it be acknowledged that mankind advanced very far in acquiring knowledge when he was still in primitive condition and there was no division among mankind. Then what was requirement of creating a Brahmin class in society? Or was it required to be Brahmin to reach at the end ultimate knowledge though discovery and progress of knowledge happened in the hands of casteless human society. Nothing is clearly understandable until it is proved how far knowledge was discovered in the hands of casteless human society and how far it happened in the hands of Brahmins. Only we can say with certainty that artificial articles were not created in the hands of Brahmins. Subsequently Indians felt little more attracted to artificial articles during dominance of Buddhism, which attraction became even more after end of Buddhism coming into contact with outer world via Islamic occupation, than what they were during Vedic period. Door to join education was totally closed before non Brahmins during Brahmin period for which material civilisation was practically absent; and very low level of education of number system and system of measurement was allowed among men, by which they could build bricks, stone made articles, Buddhist monasteries and universities during Buddhist period. Ordinary persons who are involved in regular production of articles become eager to join education if they find possibility of application of that education in work and works are less labour intensive. Such people do not feel eagerness to join education if jobs are labour dependant and there is less possibility of application of education in work. Many people during Buddhist period would join profession of masonry if brick built houses would be built for common people. They would be required to learn certain elementary level of number system and measurement for the sake of their profession. Education is required not only for invention of articles, persons who remain engaged with regular production of articles also require some level of education. Regular production of articles is not invention of articles, as articles are regularly produced by repeated performance of same production process. Articles are not regularly produced if such persons who are engaged with regular production are somehow deprived of right to get education. Remnants of ruins of cities and towns would remain as evidence till these days if brick built houses would be erected in India during Buddhist dominance. Or are old cities of India maintaining continuous unbroken run like Delhi or Kashi where remnants of ruins from old houses were used and recycled by people of subsequent generations to build their houses for which ruins of old houses of past generations are no longer available? This happens everywhere; people living in lands contiguous to ancient ruins use and recycle bricks stones etc of ruins to erect their houses. Were the old legendary cities of India, of which we learn in folklore or writings of Kalidas – Ujjain, Vidisha, Shrabasthi, Patliputra etc – continuously living cities where people in subsequent generations erected their houses removing or recycling bricks, stones etc from ruins of ancient cities for which all old cities in India were merged and intertwined in new cities and no ruin of old city is available? And where are locations of such cities if those are continuously living habitats of men? Did such cities exist during invasion of India by Muslims? Do we find mention of such cities in writings of Muslim historians? Both Kashi and Delhi are also very old cities. Many people claim that Kashi is world's oldest city as nobody knows how old it is. It could happen that there would be a very old human habitat but material civilisation did not appear. There could be a brick or stone made temple at the center surrounded by huts made of branches and leaves. People among whom knowledge was exposed built temple, but ordinary people were deprived of that knowledge. Wealth was not built among common people. Were ancient Indian cities like that where large number of people used to live but no education was circulated among them and material civilisation did not progress? We have no objection or opposition would that be so because our subject of discussion to proof is circulation of education among people and progress of civilisation. We should not suppose that civilisation flows and progresses with its own force if some people inhabit at certain place. Civilisation progresses in the hands of human beings. Civilisation progresses if ordinary people are allowed to get education. There were many localities of people in ancient India where groups of people used to live inside dense forest in primitive condition without advancement of material civilisation. But our subject of discussion is whether civilisation progressed among them or not. We can guess about whether education was circulated among common people or not by judging progress of material civilisation among such people. Civilisation of Harappa Mohenjo-Daro, which initiated at least 5000 years ago and continued till 3500 years ago, were not spread in just few central cities like Harappa Mohenjo-Daro Lothal etc; till today evidences of that civilisation, human habitation and material and other articles for consumption, have been found in more than 1000 sites on a vast land in and around Harappa Mohenjo-Daro from which it is thought that that civilisation was largest ancient civilisation. Education was circulated among people on a vast land around Harappa Mohenjo-Daro and that civilisation was spread to the extent of Rajasthan Gujarat in east. No artificial article is found in India in subsequent 1000 years till arrival of Lord Buddha. Probably people at that time used to live in huts made of branches and leaves which were dissolved in earth with time. Their other articles were earthen utensils. They might use certain metallic primary articles which used to be recycled when unusable or broken; such materials were recycled generation after generation, and probably for that reason there is no evidence of metal articles of that intermediate 1000 years. Whereas large number of articles used to be produced and circulated regularly during Harappa Mohenjo-Daro period, a large volume of which still remains as evidence, there is no evidence of material civilisation during Vedic period. It can be understood from this observation that civilisation does not move with its own force. Man forgets or is unable to learn production process of articles, and not to say invention of articles even regular production of articles stops, if circulation of education is somehow stopped among ordinary people who are actual producers and who produce articles by completing repeatedly same production process. Artificial articles are not found in India during vedic period not only in land east of Rajasthan and Gujarat but also in western India on same land mass where once thrived one great and wide spread civilisation. No evidences like cities or towns houses roads are found. It is doubtful how far activity called business or transaction was required with few numbers of articles which were in circulation in India during Brahmin or Vedic period. Probably articles which were one or two steps above those which could be produced by application of basic instincts and intuitions without any extra and acquired knowledge were in circulation. And certain elementary education, say counting from 1 to 20 and addition subtraction within that range, suitable for production of articles which were few steps above primary articles, was in circulation among common people. Education higher than that standard was not circulated among them. Probably division of profession arose in society with increase in number of articles in circulation, but that was division at its primary stage when men could perform many jobs, if not all. Men became aware of idea of private property with division of profession. Jobs in profession were simple and everybody in society could learn jobs to join profession though there was division of profession. Jobs were still simple and not heavy as no producer was required to produce huge quantity of articles to collect other articles in vogue at that time, patriarchy in its dominant form did not appear when women could still take part in jobs as works in professions were light, and population did not start to increase in those days of simple jobs though division of profession appeared in its primary form. It was possible for women to participate in economic jobs and they were not thoroughly helpless and dependant on others in those days of primary division of profession when jobs were simple and light. Patriarchy in its dominant form was absent till that time. Difference in wealth was not yet conspicuous and it is doubtful how far mankind used to feel urge to be civilized till the time of primary division of profession when everybody could join in some or other kind of economic jobs, everyone was more or less successful in his profession and was not required to join business or profession of others as workers and employees with fixed remuneration. Large numbers of articles were invented and circulated in civilized areas of western India during Harappa Mohenjo-Daro civilisation, collection and accumulation of wealth was socially accepted custom, difference in wealth was conspicuous, and there appeared higher and lower strata, probably employer and employee and even master and servant. People there felt need to be civilized or be covered with cloth. But people during Brahmin period in India did not feel urge to be civilized or be covered, or their coverage was minimal, when only very few articles were in circulation, everybody could join in some or other kind of economic jobs as a result of their simplicity and there was not much difference of wealth. People in India living in remote villages, not very long ago, say 300 to 350 years ago from now, used to remain in largely exposed condition. Large numbers of articles were created in cities and city suburbs coming into contact with Muslims, wealth was created and accumulated and difference in wealth of persons arose. Social divisions like employer employee, master servant etc were created and people felt need to be covered. But education did not advance very far in remote villages well away from cities, professions were far less in number as number of articles which people in remote villages could produce was few, jobs were simple where everybody was engaged, difference in wealth was not glaring, social strata because of difference in wealth did not rise and urge to keep distance from people in lower strata was not strong, their urge to be civilised was equally weak as they used to remain in mostly exposed condition. It is not very difficult to imagine picture during the time 3000-3500 years ago during Brahmin period when number of articles was equally few or even fewer. Wealth was created and accumulated during Harappa Mohenjo-Daro period, disputes relating to wealth arose and administrative machinery was established to settle such disputes. But what kind of administration was in force in India during Brahmin period when low volume of articles or wealth used to be created, wealth accumulation was practically absent as everyone was equally wealthy and there was no difference in wealth, everybody used to be equally successful in his profession as jobs were simple, and disputes relating to wealth were infrequent and pressure of population on wealth was low as population increase was low when women could take part in light economic jobs as number of articles was few? We do not know of any kings, queens or kingdoms of Brahmin period. Did we ever learn about any administration among red Indians of Americas who were primitive and did not see light of civilisation, in Africa south of Sahara before advent of Europeans there 400 years ago, among Jaroas and Onges in Andaman, aborigines in Australia who are presently living in Darwin province? All Indians might not be thoroughly primitive during Brahmin period. A low level of civilisation was in force among some groups of people here who used to live in small groups scattered in the land, though other people were primitive who used to live inside dense jungle and totally devoid of any knowledge to produce articles higher than most primary stage articles which could be produced by utilizing basic instincts and intuitions. This civilised people were involved in production and consumption of articles few steps above most primary articles. There used to be a section of Brahmins in every Indian community or locality, who did not take part in production of articles and used to remain detached from consumption. No education or a very low level of education was in circulation among non Brahmins in society who were involved in production of articles of consumption. Brahmins were thoroughly engaged in exercise of knowledge but how could they collect regularly most essential materials particularly food articles? Would the Brahmins produce and collect their own food? It is difficult to guess why non Brahmin producers used to supply food to Brahmins. Brahmins had no capability to give anything in return as they did not take part in production of any article. Then what was requirement to create such a strange Brahmin section keeping rest of people in dark of absence of education? It may be true that artificial articles of consumption are created, division of profession happens, difference in wealth appears and high and low strata are created in society and population increases on account of patriarchal system if education is circulated among non Brahmins. All features relating to production of artificial articles find exposure. As against this there were not many articles, difference of wealth did not rise, division of high and low strata did not happen and practically there was no division in society other than Brahmin and non Brahmin as no education or a very low level of education was allowed for common people. Population increase was absent. Even then a question always circulates in our mind what was requirement of creating such a strange Brahmin class particularly when knowledge was not discovered and progressed in the hands of Brahmins, it happened before creation of Brahmin class when mankind used to live in casteless classless society in primitive condition. It might be that Brahmins were slowly losing their unquestioned right and dominance well before end of Brahmin period or arrival of Lord Buddha, as non Brahmins were agitating and showing their anguish. Slowly non Brahmins were earning right to access to higher education and articles were invented though we find very few of their evidence. We find increasing trend of production of articles in India from beginning of Buddhism. Wealth creation and accumulation happened in India starting from that time. There appeared kings, kingdoms and administration (Kings and kingdoms were there before arrival of Lord Buddha as he himself was a prince – of that Kapilavastu. Kings and kingdoms in small scale and in primary stage appeared in Brahmin period to rule over limited number of people, as population was low in absence of large number articles to produce). One such kingdom of Puru saw rise of civilisation and advanced few steps in production of articles. They joined accumulation of wealth and attracted notice of Alexander. But can anybody say where kingdom of Puru was? Would all houses buildings even royal palace and court be made of wood which were all dissolved with time into earth? Anyway we can believe that there was a kingdom of Puru in western India where civilisation started to roll and wealth was accumulated which attracted attention of Alexander as it is written in history compiled by Greek historians. Common people were not allowed to get education or were allowed a low level of education for which we do not find brick built houses of that time though processes to manufacture bricks and building houses were known by that time to a handful number of persons. Relics of university of Takshashila, the world's oldest university built around that time are still extant. How much evidences of initial stage of Buddhism are available in India? Where were Chandragupta, Bikramaditya, Kushan Pushyamitra Shunga, Kalidas, Aryabhatta etc? Would they all live in wooden houses which were all dissolved in earth in time? It might be so, for which we do not find evidence of ancient Indian cities during early Buddhist period. All houses in legendary Indian cities next to Harappa Mohenjo-Daro, all those Patliputra, Ujjain, Vidisha, Shrabasthi etc which we find in writings of Kalidas were made of wood and there was no brick built houses. Such cities would exist during Muslim invasion and occupation would they be continuously living where people would inhabit for centuries and generations from ancient time. Many people claim that ancient city of Patliputra is present day Patna, Kanwakubja or later day Kanauj is present industrial city Kanpur, Lakmanabati or residence of Lakman, younger brother of Ram, is present day Lakhnou. We could find mention of such cities in writings of Muslim historians would they exist during occupation by Muslims. And we could find ruins of houses of ancient cities, even if those be deserted, would those be built with bricks. We do not find ruins of ancient city in India after end of Harappa Mohenjo-Daro. Nothing can be proved as no conclusion can be drawn if such cities – which we believe to be locations of ancient cities – were just simple habitats of people. Similar human localities were there everywhere in India. Rise and progress of civilisation is not proved just by existence of human habitat. Our subject of discussion is advancement of material civilisation. There might be localities of groups of people in places like Patna, Lakhnou, Kanpur etc in ancient time. Somewhat higher education was in circulation among common people and articles which were few stages above primary articles were developed during Buddhist dominance, which was mostly spread in eastern India, but it was improbable that civilisation progressed very far and surpassed or be equal to other contemporaneous civilisations in other parts of the world in creation and development of articles. But there is clear indication that wealth was created and accumulated at many places in India. Arab invader Mohammed Bin Kasim ransacked Sind province in Western India. Sultan Mahmud of Gajni invaded India many times to destroy and plunder Kashi and Somnath. Large volume of wealth used to be stored in Hindu temples. Were there no other cities or towns in India other than such temples where large volume of wealth was stored to attract attention? Would there be such wealth, that could definitely attract attention of Mahmud or similar other plunderers. Few centuries later Timur Long devastated and plundered Delhi and massacred many lakhs of people when no creature survived his attack in Delhi other than dogs and foxes during sultan rule. It is difficult to say whether there was any other principal city in India during sultan Mahmud where large wealth was accumulated. Anyway probably Brahmins started losing dominance from end of Brahmin period and non Brahmins were earning right to get higher order of education. Dominance of Brahmin was lessened to a great extent during

Buddhist period and it completely vanished during Muslim period. But Brahmins did not abandon society to live in certain suitable places, away from civilised society which was a creation out of production and consumption of artificial articles, where they could continue with their avowed profession of exercise of knowledge during the time when their dominance was lessened or after it was totally lost. They remained in this society where they joined other non Brahmins to be engaged in profession of production and distribution of articles. So Brahmins also joined in collection and consumption of articles unlike the days in the past. They had no alternative but to join in cycle of consumable articles in changed condition. The producers used to supply the Brahmins their regularly essential articles particularly food in the past during their dominance in Vedic period according to arrangement created by Brahmins. Producers used to supply the Brahmins voluntarily bucket full of food and other articles in return to regular worshiping by Brahmins and they were not required to pay any other value or exchange other articles. Also Brahmins were incapable to pay the value by any other means as they had no participation in any other economic jobs of production and exchange of articles. The Brahmins could maintain their stay in society even without collecting many articles or with limited articles during Brahmin dominance as not much education was in circulation among non Brahmins and not many articles used to be produced. People during that time did not have practice to collect many articles as very few articles were in vogue. But it was socially unacceptable or unsocial and not liked by people to continue to live in society without collecting many articles in a changed condition, when Brahmins lost dominance and non Brahmins acquired right to higher knowledge, where many articles used to be produced in society. People were aware of idea of private property and accumulation of wealth, and Brahmins had to join the same practice. Brahmins had to participate in collection and consumption of many articles forgetting age old profession of their class of exercise of knowledge. They forgot old belief that they would lose their right to get ultimate knowledge once they would join consumption of artificial articles. And during Muslim occupation probably many Brahmins joined profession of production and distribution or business of articles forgetting their traditional profession, to earn income to fulfill their intention to collect many articles to maintain equal status with others. The Brahmins, who remained, to be suitably engaged according to new arrangement, in society with new system, whose main intention was production of artificial articles of consumption, were so by name only, and not literally or in respect of work as the name of their class might suggest. In our time the real Brahmins are those naked ascetics living in high altitude of the Himalaya and thoroughly engaged in exercise of knowledge and detached with consumption and enjoyment of articles.

It is clear that mankind was able to invent and develop artificial articles only when it became acquainted with number system and invented system of measurement. But why only non Brahmins should be held responsible for creation of artificial articles? Or why should they share full credit for that? Civilisation appeared and progressed in all those Greece Rome west Asia America wherever men became acquainted with number system. But we never knew of caste division like Brahmin non Brahmin in societies in such lands. Caste system was there in Greece Rome west Asia before Christ as long as paganism was dominant custom, as caste ism was there in central and west Asia before introduction of Islam. But that caste division was result of production process of artificial articles. Jobs in those days were exclusively dependant on physical strength. Demand for articles were created among mankind when such articles were produced after invention, everybody in society was eager to consume but who would produce? It was time of all pervading physical strength, mechanization of job was a far cry at that time, not a possibility even in dreams. Educated people in those days of all pervading physical strength did not become eager to join production of articles which were in circulation among mankind. But jobs must be accomplished so that articles could be produced, otherwise how articles could reach man and his demand was satisfied if these were not produced? Finally jobs were destined to be done by ill educated people of society. The ill educated people used to be engaged in production of articles, such articles could reach men or customer as a result of physical labour of such persons, and men could get opportunity to consume articles. But such ill educated producing people used to remain in lower strata of society. Educated people never used to take part in such physically laborious jobs. At best they would be owners of workshops producing articles or would join trading business of such articles. But they never used to join production of articles. Long before that idea of profit and loss in business was recognized in society. Many people who were unsuccessful in their own profession used to join workshops of other people at fixed remuneration. Owners used to earn larger volume of profit by selling in market increased volume of articles manufactured by workers; owners themselves alone could not produce so much. There happened glaring difference of possessed wealth in society. Many people became poor. On the one hand such workers in workshops belonging to others were uneducated, on the other they were poor, so they found their place at lower strata of society. Doors of temples of paganism in those days were closed before such people, living in lower strata of society, who could not contribute any amount for worship in temples. They lost their right to join in religious activities. Everybody should have right to pray to god, but that right of people living in lower strata was snatched as they were poor and unable to contribute to worship in temple. Caste division was created among civilized people in those days on account of production of artificial articles. Christianity, Islam or other popular modern religions were introduced to regain right of religious activities of people in lower strata eradicating caste division and uniting all people on a common platform of casteless religion. Caste divisions were there in society before introduction of religion to indicate upper or lower strata, but Brahmin non Brahmin division was absent. Caste division was a creation of industrialization and physically laborious nature of production process of articles in other civilisations outside India. It was not similar to Brahmin non Brahmin division in India. Brahmin non Brahmin division in India during Vedic period was a strange one; it was a division to deprive one section of people from getting education. It was not a division to deprive and exploit economically any group of people, as there was few numbers of articles during Brahmin period when jobs in workshops were not heavy and nobody used to fail in profession to join other's workshops as workers to be exploited. Deprivation and exploitation can happen in a situation of large number of articles when jobs in professions become heavy where many people become unsuccessful in professions to join professions of others as workers where they can be exploited. It is a myth that Indian society was corrupt with caste division during Brahmin period and also subsequent Buddhist period when lower caste people were deprived and exploited. Few numbers of articles were in circulation during those periods where everybody was more or less successful in his profession in which it was not possible to exploit any group of people. Exploitation and deprivation started on Indian soil after Muslim domination when there happened production of large number of articles, and caste division became a feature of Indian society. Caste division was a creation to deprive section of people in the course of production of articles, it is a means to exploit lower caste people. It is unthinkable that caste division can exist in society where there are not many articles to produce which does not allow opportunity to certain section of people to exploit other. Caste division created in relation to production of articles is not similar to division like Brahmin non Brahmin as later division has no relation to production. Caste division was there in both of Americas in civilized people, even slave system was there, which were outcomes of production process of artificial articles though no religion was introduced there to unite all people. Caste division and slave system were very distinctly present in cities and localities of both of Americas when the Spanish invaded and occupied Americas. Artificial articles were created in societies without any division like Brahmin non Brahmin in lands outside India. Once upon a time such articles were created in India before creation of Brahmin during Harappa Mohenjo-Daro, and subsequently these were not created in the hands of Brahmins during Brahmin dominance. We can reach to one conclusion from all such events that society without division like Brahmin non Brahmin is most suitable ground for creation of articles. Brahmins do not create articles during their dominance. It is wrong to say that non Brahmins are responsible or claimant for credit of creation of artificial articles.

Civilisations at Greece Rome west Asia Egypt provide evidences against the argument that artificial articles are achievement of non Brahmins. We find acquaintance with number system and creation of articles from very beginning of these civilisations. We can imagine noticing such facts that number system was revealed in a casteless society and artificial articles were initially created in the hands of people of such society. Relics of first civilisation of Europe, which appeared in Crete island of Greece 2000 years ago before Christ, ruins of articles, houses, palaces etc, are still extant. Definitely they were aware of number system during that time or before that. But did they become aware of number system independently or by virtue of their contact with some other people? Their history before civilisation is not clear and full of mystery. Rome civilisation used to imitate Greece from very beginning (around 750 BC), initially almost everything they learnt from Greece. We can infer that Rome was not origin for discovery of number system. We find evidence of artificial articles from beginning of Egyptian civilisation (around 3100 BC). History before that is mysterious. Wherefrom did they learn knowledge of number system? Did they learn it independently or acquired that knowledge from somewhere else? There is no proof for either. Nowhere else there is distinctly clear division of Brahmin non Brahmin as it is in India. That is why our doubt becomes even deeper rooted whether Brahmins were required to learn number system or non Brahmins were equally capable to do that. This doubt will continue until it is clearly proved that number system was discovered particularly by either Brahmins or non Brahmins and thereafter it spread everywhere all over the world, though it spread among all irrespective of caste or creed while being transmitted everywhere else and many people became eager to create artificial articles.

Was number system added in store of knowledge of India after introduction of Buddhism and material civilisation progressed here if we intend to suppose that number system was not there in knowledge bank of India and for that reason material civilisation did not initiate here before Buddhist era? There is no reason to infer like that. Not only that there was mathematics in Vedas, people here came to learn number long before introduction of Buddhism during Harappa Mohenjo-Daro civilisation, and large scale material civilisation was built there. Was that knowledge lost thereafter along with Harappa Mohenjo-Daro? Did people forget to join its study? Or it continued for generations to remain in circulation during formation of Vedas Upanishads? Probably all people did not join that study, but some used to join it. Particularly nothing could be added in Vedas, those remained unchanged for millenniums, as these books were held traditionally with high esteem by people. So, mathematics was there in Vedas well before introduction of Buddhism. Volumes of knowledge particularly that of mathematics was not suddenly added in Indian store of knowledge just next to introduction of Buddhism by which it was possible to initiate material civilisation of artificial articles. This knowledge was there in India before introduction of that religion. It was possible that ordinary people earned right to get education, of which they were deprived so long. But it is also not true that there came a sea change in Indian society just after introduction of that religion. We find only Buddhist monasteries here and there at many places, but no proliferation of evidence of other articles.

Who can say with certainty how old is knowledge of number system and Vedas? Were artificial articles invented and circulated on a vast land starting from Rajasthan in India and comprising west Asia and even after that Sahara in Africa, patriarchal system appeared as a result of laborious production process of such articles and population increased at explosive rate which resulted in massacre of crores of people in a greater Indian world war, as is narrated in Indian epic the Mahabharata, as a result of exposure of number system? Many scholars believe that deserts in west Asia and North Africa are manmade and not natural. It is believed that once upon a time such vast deserts were fertile lands and inhabited by large number of people. We can reach a definite conclusion that mankind became aware of number system before that larger Indian world war if it really happened to reduce huge pressure of population. Answers to all these questions are shrouded in mystery, and nothing can be known clearly. But our principal subject of discussion is origin of number system. We can reach certain common laws and conclusions from social behaviour of human groups scattered all over the world which we came across in our effort to find evidence of artificial articles. First we can find all over the world evidence of most primary articles and weapons. We can find such evidence even among human groups living in inaccessible lands. But we find evidence of more improved next stage articles among those human groups only among whom knowledge of number was exposed. We can infer from such facts that no particular and extra knowledge was required to invent such primary articles. Mankind found and produced such articles with his congenital basic instincts and intuitions. But better quality and next stage materials are found among those human groups only who became acquainted with number. We do not find evidence of next stage and better improved articles among people who live in far off inaccessible land without contact with outside world, for which they are unable to acquire knowledge of number from outside, but they cannot independently discover number. Even now they are confined among few primary articles, and did not advance further. We can reach a conclusion, coming to this stage, that no particular and extra knowledge is required to invent and produce most primary stage articles. Man can produce such articles utilizing his elementary instincts. But only those human groups could produce next stage and more improved articles among whom knowledge, particularly that of number was exposed. But here there is another doubt. All people, who became aware of knowledge, did not join production of articles. Most civilisations in the world are dependent on material, those civilisations were initiated, prospered and spread circling around invention production and distribution of artificial articles. And articles which were produced during such civilisations could not be produced without knowledge of number and measurement system. People became aware of knowledge of number before initiation of civilisation. People were acquainted with number in civilisations of Sumer Egypt Greece Rome etc wherever we find extensive use of artificial articles. But material civilisation did not progress in few places even when people there were aware of knowledge of number such as in India. We can infer from this fact that material civilisation did not prosper in land and among people where education was restricted in the hands of Brahmin priests and higher castes, and not circulated among all, though certain section of people were aware of knowledge. Brahmin priests nowhere created artificial articles. Material civilisation progressed only in those lands where ordinary people were allowed to get education. Brahmins and priests were thoroughly engaged in exercise of knowledge to reach highest order of knowledge, they never abandoned that exercise or diverted from that avowed target. Only non Brahmins who were allowed to get education had no commitment to reach highest order and they used to end education at certain intermediate stage and used to produce articles utilizing their acquired knowledge. Material civilisation progressed in their hands.

(2)

Mankind therefore continued to produce artificial articles. Initially there was few number of articles. All people then used to produce all articles unitedly. Nobody used to feel much difficulty in learning production processes of all articles and produce those as number of articles was few. All people used to divide produced articles equally among themselves as all used to join in production. There was no difference in wealth as all produced articles used to be divided equally and all used to possess same amount of wealth. There was no need to acquire any wealth with individual effort as there was no difference in division of produced articles and everybody used to get equal share. Nobody was aware of idea of private property. Even now idea of private property is not known by members of primitive groups of people who are still living in different corners of earth in primitive condition among whom many articles were not invented.

Number of artificial articles was not stagnant in human society. Its number was increasing as man was inventing new articles. Number of articles one day became so large that it was not possible for all people to learn production processes of all articles. Division of profession happened as a result of increase in number of articles when all people were unable to produce all articles. All people selected their professions, as smiths, potters, carpenters etc, but men were not satisfied in consuming articles produced in their own professions, they were eager to enjoy articles produced in professions of others also. Smith used to show interest in earthen utensils produced by potters, carpenters used to be interested in building materials and the likes. Everyone was required to collect materials produced by others in exchange of own produced articles. That was the beginning of business as a result of increase in number of articles of consumption. If somebody thinks that business was started among mankind from desire to amass wealth or enjoy more, that thought is wrong. Activity called business was initiated among mankind as a result of increase in number of articles, when it was not possible for all people to produce all articles. Business or transaction would not initiate if all people could produce their required articles.

All people used to join to produce all articles unitedly as long as number of articles was few. Any particular method of selection of profession or article for production was till that time unknown to mankind. It was not probable that society helped or advised men in selection of profession for production of particular article on account of increase in number. Rather everyone selected his own profession. Some people became engaged in production of certain articles where they found deficiency in supply compared to demand. There appeared another problem when everybody selected his own profession. Everyone possessed equal wealth and there was no difference in wealth as long as all people used to produce unitedly and divide all articles equally among themselves. There was no possibility of emergence of idea of private property. But now everyone was required to decide how much articles one would intend to produce in one's profession. Those who used to produce large volume of articles could collect large volume of articles produced in other professions in exchange of own produced articles. Many other producers, who produced low volume of articles in their own profession, used to remain satisfied with less quantity of other articles. Persons who were unsuccessful in their own profession joined professions of others as employees. Now there appeared difference in possessed wealth and men became aware of idea of private property. People did not share excess wealth with other fellow members of community, rather they used to enjoy excess wealth themselves. Custom of equal division of produced material among members of community ended with division of profession which happened as a result of increase in number of articles. Difference in possessed wealth did not become large and conspicuous just on division of profession. Number of articles was not very large at initial stage of division of profession. It was little more than number which allowed men to work and produce unitedly. People divided in professions, but even then everybody was required to produce limited volume of articles which could be sufficient to enable him to collect other articles as number of articles was limited. Jobs in professions did not become heavy where even women could take part in production, and they did not become absolutely helpless and dependant. Patriarchal system did not become firmly aground and population did not increase painfully. Every person or producer was successful in his own profession as jobs in professions were easy to perform in a situation of few numbers of articles, and each of them could collect other articles of consumption in exchange of limited volume of articles produced in his own profession. Volume of articles produced was sufficient to meet total demand of society and pressure of population on property or wealth was not heavy to lead men to many disputes. Many persons were not forced to join antisocial activities to collect their required materials, being unsuccessful in professions. Administration among mankind at that time of initial division of profession was not very busy in settling disputes of members of community relating to private property or to protect private property from theft and robbery by unsuccessful people who used to join antisocial activities to collect articles of consumption. All people were more or less equally successful in their professions as long as number of articles was few for which jobs in professions were easy and light, and nobody was forced to join crimes, being unsuccessful in professions, to keep administration busy in controlling crimes. India during Brahmin and Buddhist period provides us with certain instances that population does not increase agonizingly as long as number of articles are few when everybody is more or less equally successful in producing articles of his profession and collecting articles produced by other producers as jobs in professions remain easy and light because each producer is required to produce limited quantity of articles which can be sufficient to enable him to collect other articles in circulation in society which are few in number. Women also can take part in jobs, and patriarchy does not become dominant. That time in initial stage of division of profession administration was mostly busy in protecting property of members of community from primitive people who used to live in close proximity of civilised people but did not join civilisation, but who used to be lured by wealth of civilised people to intend to snatch such wealth. Administration and legal system were at their elementary forms in initial stage of division of profession. But this difference in possessed wealth of persons became bigger and glaring when number of articles of consumption became larger for which jobs in professions became heavier, many persons who were unsuccessful in their own professions joined professions of others as workers, and owners of such professions could collect even bigger volume of wealth by selling in market larger volume of product which they alone could not produce. Number of articles of consumption did not remain stagnant at a particular point and was increasing continuously though with long gap. Persons engaged in production of articles were required to produce larger volume of articles in their professions to enable themselves to collect many articles which were invented and circulated. Jobs in professions became difficult and heavier where many producers failed to achieve success in their professions. Also women became unable to take part in jobs in certain capacities to perform lighter parts of jobs when such jobs became heavy as a result of increase in number of articles. Patriarchal order became dominant social custom with increase in number of articles when women were judged incapable to join jobs and became dependant on men. Population started increasing. Pressure of population increased on limited volume of wealth produced. Many people failed to achieve success in professions when jobs in professions became heavier and difficult as a result of increase in number of articles as each producer was required to produce larger volume of articles which could be required to enable him to collect many other varieties of articles. Many of such unsuccessful persons joined professions of other successful producers as workers with fixed remuneration and not as partners with right of equal share in profit.

Volumes of articles produced in workshops of successful producers were multiplied when many persons joined their workshops as workers. Producers alone could not produce that much volume of articles. A person, however great engineer, doctor or worker he be, can produce very limited quantity of articles or complete limited volume of service with his individual capacity. He can earn limited amount of revenue by selling such limited volume of articles or services in market. But volume of such articles and services can multiply if he appoints few numbers of persons in his workshop. He can earn larger revenue by selling such larger volume of articles and services in market. But owner of workshop retains larger amount of profit for himself and distributes only salary at fixed rate among employees. Difference in possessed wealth of persons became large and eye catching when many unsuccessful persons in their own professions as a result of increase in number of articles joined others' workshops as workers which enabled owners of such workshops to earn larger profit and amass wealth. Pressure of population became heavier on produced articles and there happened many disputes relating to private property as rate of increase in produced articles failed to match rate of increase in population. Particularly area of residential and cultivable lands could not be increased to a greater extent with increase in population. Many unsuccessful persons in their professions joined antisocial activities to collect required materials. Administration became busy to settle disputes among mankind and protect property of inhabitants in society, when such disputes and crimes increased in number as a result of increase in number of articles, for which jobs in professions became heavy and difficult which forced many people to become unsuccessful in professions. Requirement of administration and legal system was felt more with increase in number of articles.

Business or transaction initiated among mankind as a result of increase in number of articles. Gradually there appeared other features of production and business of articles. Number of articles was increasing continuously though with long gap. People used to take part initially in barter system of transaction as long as number of articles was within a manageable limit to conveniently join in system of exchange of material. But number of articles was not stagnant there, it became even larger. There are certain inconveniences in barter system or exchange of materials, both parties have to bring their materials at certain common place where they determine exchange rate by bargain. But greater inconvenience is that medium of exchange changes every time a transaction takes place and it becomes difficult to determine rate of exchange. When a smith and a potter join in exchange then mediums are metallic dagger hoe axe on one side and earthen pitchers and bowls on the other. When the same smith joins in exchange with a carpenter then mediums are metallic articles and wooden furniture. This inconvenience of change of medium of exchange became multiplied in prehistoric time with increase in number of articles. First certain food article which was essential and widely used by all people, suppose rice, was selected as common medium of exchange to overcome this difficulty of determining rate of exchange. Every producer had to determine volume of rice as value of his produced articles. But problem of medium of exchange was not totally removed by selecting certain food article as medium. This food article as medium was required to be carried every time any exchange took place. But number of articles was increasing continuously and with that number of exchange was also increasing. Everybody was expecting certain medium of exchange which was small in size easy to carry and count. So idea of money was created among mankind as common medium of exchange as a result of increase in number of articles. Business or transaction became easier with introduction of money as common medium of exchange as it helped easy determination of value of articles. Circulation of legal tender money as common medium of exchange required that certain marks of administrators were impressed on articles circulated as money. Initially shells and later metallic coins were used as money. Then fishermen who were regularly engaged in fishing activity when shells from under water could be netted, and smiths who regularly produced metal articles could be richest persons in society if no mark was required. By that time administration was already instituted as many numbers of articles were in circulation and mankind felt need to introduce administration to protect properties of members of society. Some articles similar to money or common medium of exchange were thought of and initiated among few closed groups of persons or businessmen before being circulated as common medium to be circulated in entire community, just like many other things which were first initiated among small groups of persons, who first started production of that article or service, to be ultimately accepted by whole society. Administrations in those days advocated this idea of easily countable and transportable money in the form of shells and coins, first introduced and circulated among small but closely held and trusted groups of persons, as small and easily transportable medium of exchange to be circulated in entire community, after being impressed with certain marks of administrators to give them legality. By this time profit and loss in business was approved by society. Many persons who became unsuccessful in own profession joined others' profession as workers which helped owners of such workshops to amass wealth. As men used to select their own profession and society had no say in that selection and society could not make any arrangement for those who were unable to select any profession or were unsuccessful in their profession, similarly producers used to determine prices of their products and society had no control over that. Everybody used to accumulate wealth according to one's capacity. Producers or owners of professions, who were successful and could employ many other persons, could amass wealth and there appeared glaring difference in possessed wealth, which led to disputes relating to private property among members.

Need for marking of property was felt first when men became aware of private property as a result of division of profession, not just at the time of amassing of wealth. Properties can move and does not remain stationery just by verbal declaration of possession by somebody. People remaining surrounding and contiguous to any particular land can grab parts of that land to increase their own holding. Precinct can still be erected around lands resided by people which are in most cases small in area, but cultivable lands which are far bigger remain unmarked to indicate possession by any person. It becomes difficult to determine land cultivated by any cultivator at the time of harvesting in every season which results in disputes and sometimes in bloody scuffle. Need for marking private property was felt when this idea of private property appeared among mankind. This need was not so much felt when number of articles was few, slightly above the threshold which allowed men to work conjointly, when works in professions were not that heavy to disallow women to work and population did not increase. Pressure of population on property was not heavy to force men to be involved in many disputes. But this need was felt more seriously when number of articles increased which made jobs in professions heavy to disallow women to take part in work and population increased for which there was heavier pressure on property, which led men to many disputes. Written document as proofs and notifications were needed to indicate possession by particular persons. So was created law. It generally contains detail discussion in written form about how and in what different manners a person can get title over a property. It also contains detail instruction of necessary documents a person is required to collect to maintain possession on any property. There used to be disputes brawls scuffles relating to property among mankind before creation of law. It was created to prevent people from such disputes and scuffles. Root cause of creation of law is also increase in number of artificial articles of consumption for which there appeared private property where from were started disputes. And branch of knowledge called law was created and initiated among those human groups only where non Brahmin ordinary people were allowed to get education for which many articles were invented. Human groups who live in inaccessible lands far away from civilized society and who have no contact with civilized world and are unaware of any knowledge are still existing with few number of articles which man can invent and produce utilizing his basic instincts and intuitions without any extra acquired knowledge, and does not progress further. Only few numbers of articles of consumption are in vogue among them which they produce unitedly and divide equally. Division of profession did not appear among them and they are unaware of idea private property even till this day. Women in primitive societies take part in works along with men to produce and collect few numbers of articles which are in vogue there. Their participation in production and collection is never objected. As they join in production and collection, so they claim equal share along with male members in produced and collected articles. They are not helpless and dependant on anybody and does not approve dominance by men. Patriarchal dominance is absent in primitive society and population increase is not experienced there. Population pressure on produced and collected materials is absent to induce men to join in brawl to get fair share of articles. Volume of produced and collected articles is sufficient for distribution among limited number of persons in primitive society. There is no private property and population pressure on articles to prompt people to join in disputes is absent, so law was not created as its need was not felt. Disputes or scuffles relating to private property do not happen among them. Branch of knowledge called law was not created among primitive people living in primitive condition inside Amazon jungle in South America, in Darwin state of Australia, in different corners of Africa, Polynesian islands, Bastar district of Chhattisgarh and Medak and Malkangiri districts of Orissa, as it is not required.

Law does not oppose private property. We shall have to go back to prehistoric time stopping production and distribution of all articles if we intend to do that. In addition to that we should stop circulation of education among all non Brahmin people. No artificial articles can be created and division of profession and private property do not appear if that much is done. Rather law advocates both individual enterprise and property. It has been created to regulate behaviour among people in relation to private property. Men no longer remained claimant and possessor of any property anywhere as per his wish. He is required to follow legal procedure to establish his claim on any property. Probably man showed such tendency before formation and introduction of law. They used to be eager and claim to possess any property anywhere, sometimes by force. Particularly that happened when there happened increased pressure on property as a result of population increase. That used to originate many disputes and even scuffles.

Private properties appeared in some parts of India during Harappa Mohenjo-Daro as artificial articles were developed. Many articles of consumption were created and material civilisation initiated and progressed. We can guess that some kind of law and order was created to enact and ensure private properties of men though there is no proof of that. Evidences of written materials of Harappa Mohenjo-Daro whatever have been found could not be deciphered till today and language of that land is unknown. There descended a period of unknown void in India just next to Harappa Mohenjo-Daro time. We do not find evidence of any city town locality king kingdom etc of that time. But evidence is present about exposure of knowledge in India at that time. Vedas Brahmin Upanishads Puranas Ramayana Mahabharata all were there at that time of void, but not to say of any city or town even no artificial articles of that time is found. We can guess that ordinary non Brahmins were not allowed to get education and no artificial article was created here in that span of 1000 years of void. Production processes of articles of which people became aware during Harappa Mohenjo-Daro period were lost in subsequent period as ordinary people were denied right to get education. Only Brahmins had right to acquire education. But they never created any artificial articles, only purpose of their exercise of education was to reach highest order of knowledge. Rest non Brahmins were allowed a very low order of education by which they could produce few more number of articles slightly better than most primary articles, and other people were primitive living inside jungles without access to any education, and among whom there were no articles next to stage of articles which could be produced by application of elementary instincts and intuitions. Large number of articles, division of profession and idea of private property did not appear among them. So creation of law was not felt during that 1000 years of void in India. Ordinary people utilized their acquired education to create artificial articles, people became aware of idea of private property and creation and circulation of law was felt there to settle disputes relating to private property wherever education was circulated among all in a casteless society.

Law was created with intention to enact, control and regulate behavoiur of mankind in relation to private property. There might be some kind of law among mankind even before creation of private property for regulating some other social behaviour, such as marital relation. It was sage Uddalak according to Indian Puranas and Mahabharata who first gave law of social custom called marriage in the world. Before that there was no particular relation like marriage between male and female and no institution called family. We find same kind of social custom called marriage and family throughout the world, as it is found even among primitive people. We find it even among people living in inaccessible land and without any contact with outside world, though unwritten. Who preached and introduced law of marriage among people in inaccessible land where men from civilised world cannot reach? Did this law spread in the whole world when it was preached by sage Uddalak, even in far corners of world, or human groups in different places independently learnt and introduced this law among themselves without help from outside? Law of marriage is same throughout the world. But it is improbable that people living in far away and inaccessible land without contact with outside world came to learn about law of marriage coming into contact with civilized world. They were aware of this law even before coming into contact with civilized world in recent past. Now we have no opportunity to know who introduced law of marriage in different parts of the world; whether it was introduced by a particular person from where it was circulated throughout the world or human groups in different parts independently introduced it among themselves.

Law was therefore created to keep a control on human behaviour relating to private property. Its need was felt only when people became aware of idea of private property as a result of division of profession which happened on account of increase in number of articles of consumption. Subsequently many other laws were created to exercise control over human behaviour in other fields of activities, such as religious activities. Religion was created and introduced much later, though it was also created in relation to artificial articles of consumption. It was found during production of artificial articles after their creation and introduction that people who were somewhat educated in society would not take part in production. That was a period of all pervading physical strength. Muscle strength was most essential for producing any article. There used to remain a large section of population in society to perform such jobs. Their level of education was very low. Educated people never used to take part in physically laborious production process. By that time employment of people in workshop and earning profit were approved by society, or more precisely unsuccessful persons in professions used to join workshops of successful producers which could enable such successful producers to earn larger profit. Producers, who were successful in business of production and distribution of articles, used to employ few employees to increase volume of articles produced in their workshops, income of business also used to be increased, but proprietors owners used to retain larger share of revenue and only fixed salary used to be allotted among employees at the time of distribution of revenue. These ill educated and poor people engaged with physically laborious low income jobs found their accommodation in lowest strata in society. They were even forbidden to enter temples and other places of worships. Caste ism appeared in all those materialistic civilisations whose roots were aground in production of artificial articles. Existence of this group of people was inevitable in society, it was not possible to manufacture artificial articles without them. But they had no respectable position in society. At certain point of time religion was initiated among those civilisations where caste division appeared as a result of production process of articles, particularly to regain right of lower caste people to worship. All modern religions have same purpose, re-empowering people in lower strata to worship. There need not be separate Islamic law, Christian law or Buddhist law when purpose of all these modern religions is same. Private property appeared from artificial articles, and law was created to regulate manner of consumption and enjoyment of articles by men. Picture is same throughout the world. If we take into consideration profit or loss in business - is it earned in certain way in Christian society and in a different way in Islamic society? All over the world ways and means to earn profit and incur loss is same – higher profit is earned by employing many people in workshop to increase volume of product and selling increased product in market to earn higher revenue, but retaining profit by owner only and distributing fixed salary among employees as employees do not share equally in profit with owners. Can any religion show that their members behave differently when number of articles increases? People all over the world show same tendency in similar situation, when they divide among professions, become aware and conscious of idea of private property and introduce administration to protect their properties. They do not share extra earned wealth with other members of society, rather they keep such wealth for own consumption. They even dominate women when women become unable to join jobs for physically strenuous nature of jobs and men folk take this opportunity of helpless condition of women to increase population. All over the world people take part in business to collect many articles which they cannot produce themselves and they even introduce and circulate legal tender money for ease of transaction. They do not show restraint to remain detached from earthly pleasure avoiding articles of consumption. If religions want to differ in formulation of legal system, they can better urge their members to join equal distribution of articles, as was customary before division of profession, even in a situation of large number of articles. All members of community should divide in groups to produce certain particular articles unitedly by group members and deposit such articles at center of community, from where everybody should pick up his or her required articles. Nobody should be questioned about his or her right to pick up required articles, as engagement of any person in certain work should entitle him or her to pick up articles. Even women should be allowed to get required materials. Then there can be equal distribution of wealth. Also their members should share equally revenue of professions even when unsuccessful persons in their own professions join professions of successful persons. After all owners of such professions cannot themselves, with their individual capacity, produce the volume of articles produced by their employees, however successful owners they can be. There can be one common legal system in the whole world as people all over the world behave in similar way and show same tendency while utilizing articles of consumption. It is useless or unnecessary to have different legal systems in different areas or among people following different religions or social customs.

Legal system was created in those countries and among those nations only where materialistic civilisation appeared. It was felt to create legal system to mark private property and to enact and regulate ways and means to help possess such property by people, so that their possession could be smooth and trouble free. Also it was created to discourage unjustified claim on property. Idea of private property was not germinated among people who did not see creation of large number of articles and they did not feel necessity to build any legal system to regulate possession and use of such property. Many people complain that no legal system was found in ancient India unlike other ancient civilisations where evidences of it are still extant. But we should inquire whether any civilisation in relation to artificial materials appeared and progressed very far in India before making such complain. Harappa Mohenjo-Daro civilisation was spread up to Rajasthan Gujarat. Probably land up to these two states was converted to desert as a result of increase in population among civilized people as works were dependant on muscle power. Is desert in Rajasthan Gujarat and further west natural or manmade? Many scholars believe that desert in west Asia is manmade and not natural. A large land mass was converted into desert as outcome of making it cultivable to grow more food to support increased population by removing forest cover leading to lack of rain when that land experienced population increase. Even Sahara the largest desert may be like that. Archeologists have found dried bed of river in Sahara; there are still few lakes, which have no connection with any other water body or river in the vicinity, along the course of the dead river inside desert, but in one such lake there are few crocodiles as last evidence of a live river in the past. There are many evidences of human habitation in the past inside Sahara desert. All deserts on earth are not manmade. Most of areas in inner land mass in Australia are arid for which no city was founded inside the continent and all cities are beside the sea. But the continent is surrounded by oceans which can form cloud to pour rain throughout it, and added with that no civilisation was ever initiated in Australia at any time during human history and there was never any population increase so that large tracts of lands could be denuded of forest cover to convert it to arid land. But there is a huge and natural arid zone inside the continent. The deadly Kalahari Desert in South Africa is not very far from the Atlantic Ocean and Namib Desert in Namibia is just beside the Atlantic. But these areas do not experience rain. There also no civilisation appeared ever during human history and population did not increase to remove forest cover. Same is the case with Atacama Desert in Chile. So it is a fact that deserts are created by natural process. But it is also possible that reason for creation of some deserts was human folly. Can we imagine that Harappa Mohenjo-Daro Lothal civilisation was spread till Rajasthan Gujarat, population here increased profusely and the land was converted to desert in the course of time for large scale removal of forest cover? If land around Harappa Mohenjo-Daro was once cultivable which became desert like as a result of large scale removal of forest cover, then we can guess large scale increase of population in that land and strong presence of dominant patriarchal order. Large number of articles used to be produced there and works in workshops were heavy and physically laborious which disqualified women to participate in work when they became helplessly dependant on men to accept patriarchal dominance. Population pressure on limited volume of wealth and property increased which forced men to be involved in many disputes. Also many persons became unsuccessful in profession to join crimes to collect required materials as jobs in professions became heavier and difficult with increase in number of articles. People there felt for administration and legal system to settle property related disputes and protect property of inhabitants. It is reasonable to think that legal system was formed among inhabitants of this large land as civilisation initiated and progressed there to a great extent, they became aware of idea of private property and everybody was busy to accumulate property. There was an administrative machinery to enforce legal system so that people's possession of property could be smooth and trouble free. Kind of legal system in force in Harappa Mohenjo-Daro is not known, their written script has not till been deciphered. Varieties and large volume of evidence indicating legal system have been found in Egypt, Sumer, Urr, Akkad, Assyria or in later day Persepolis, like writings on wall and legal edicts inscribed in earthen tablets. Such evidences are more conspicuous and voluminous in case of later day Greece and Rome. Roman laws are studied even in these days in schools and colleges, and not many words are required to prove that there was a strongly established roman legal system.

We can guess large scale increase in population and even before that creation of many articles, rise of awareness of private property among people, appearance of patriarchal dominance in society in all those centers of civilisations, spread on a vast land in west Asia starting from Rajasthan Gujarat in India which have ultimately been converted into desert. But what was picture in India next to sudden disappearance of Harappa Mohenjo-Daro civilisation? Indian history during 1000 years next to Harappa Mohenjo-Daro before arrival of Lord Buddha and Mahabir Jain is full of mystery, nothing is known clearly, only evidences we learn are Vedas Upanishads Ramayana Mahabharata etc. Which era did Kalidas and Bikramaditya belong to, where were Patliputra, Ujjain? Do we find any material evidence? Harappa Mohenjo-Daro are 5000 years old, we can guess that Patliputra Ujjain were at least 2500 years old. Why cannot we get evidence of 2500 year old ruins while remnants of 5000 year old ruins are still distinctly extant? Can it be so that these legendary Indian cities are always living during last 2500 years and new habitats were built over or utilizing ruins of earlier materials for which evidence of earlier cities are all lost whereas ruins of Harappa Mohenjo-Daro are still extant as these are dead cities and no new city was built on old ruins? Old cities are still lying under new cities?

We cannot reach any definite conclusion until old cities are excavated and material evidences are available. Till that time all these cities are part of folk lore and poetic imagination. Rome, Athens, Crete island these are also living cities starting from ancient past, there remnants of ruins of old cities, as evidence of ancient civilisation, are still existing. But only in this India modern cities were always built just right on evidences, like temples, royal living courts, forts etc, of ancient civilisation? Anyway we have at last reached a conclusion that there is no material evidence during intermediate period of 1000 years next to Harappa Mohenjo-Daro and before arrival of Lord Buddha, and evidence of articles during subsequent Buddhist period is not that great to evince advancement and proliferation of material civilisation. We do not find article belonging to Brahmin period other than some earthen materials; and some materials here and there in the form of monasteries and universities, but not materials utilized by men, during Buddhist period are available. And entire India east of Rajasthan Gujarat was full of jungle and water bodies before arrival of Muslims, not to speak of cities and towns. Western India, where once a great civilisation thrived, was also desert like during Vedic period without progress of civilisation. There is no proof of population increase during that time of 1000 years. Large land is made cultivable by removing forest cover to grow larger volume of food to support larger population as a result of increase in number of people. Land covered with jungle is proof that population did not increase. Artificial articles were not created in large number in India and patriarchy did not appear here as there was no laborious job here in absence of production of large number of articles. Works in workshops were light as every producer was required to produce limited volume of articles which could be sufficient to enable him to collect other articles which were few in number. There were small groups of men comprising of Brahmins and some non Brahmins during Brahmin period in India. Brahmins only had right of education. But they used to join education with a commitment to reach highest order of knowledge and never would be eager to create artificial articles by ending education at certain intermediate stage. Other people in society were allowed a very low level of education and could produce few articles slightly higher in levels above primary articles. Other people in this land were primitive living in jungle. Not many articles were there and so there production process or laborious jobs were absent in this land, dominant patriarchy did not appear here and population did not increase. Division of profession and idea of private property were in their initial stage, all people could easily learn some or other production process. All people were engaged in profession and were successful. Difference in wealth of people was not conspicuous, in fact there was not much creation and accumulation of wealth in absence of large number of articles during Brahmin period. Deficiency in supply of wealth did not happen as population did not increase, there was sufficient wealth for limited number of people. awareness to idea of private property was there in its initial stage as number of articles was just higher than threshold which could allow men to produce conjointly as was customary among primitive people, but not many disputes used to arise as there was sufficient supply of articles compared to total demand, population was low and pressure of population on property to force men to join in disputes was equally low. Also tendency of men to join crime to collect required materials was low as most of the people used to be successful in professions as jobs in professions were easy and light in a situation of few numbers of articles. People did not feel powerful urge to enact law. Administrative system in India during Brahmin period is shrouded in mystery and not clearly known. Some kind of legal system might be here in India in its most primary stage without many components and stringent strictures. Indian law might be a general description of human behaviour in relation to possession and enjoyment of property unlike law in other lands where it contained more specific instructions to act in different situations. Of course people in India during that time with very few numbers of articles did not encounter many situations in relation to behaviour of man in connection to private property. A law with many components and branches was not required. Situation during Buddhist period was not very different. Slightly higher level of education than was in circulation among common people during Brahmin period was allowed for such people, and as a result number of articles increased than was in vogue during Brahmin period, but did not become so large to make works in workshops heavy and difficult to exclude women from work places. Women in India were not that helplessly inactive to depend thoroughly on men for subsistence. Population here did not increase painfully even during Buddhist period. Population pressure on articles for consumption was not heavy, or in other words, volume of produced articles was sufficient to match total demand of society, people were largely free from disputes to get fair share of articles, which disputes would happen would there be pressure on limited volume of articles. Also works in professions were still not that heavy during Buddhist period as number of articles was not very large. People were more or less successful in professions and collecting required articles and were not inclined to join crimes. Administrations in India during Brahmin and Buddhist periods were mostly busy in protecting properties of inhabitants of civilised societies from theft and robbery committed by primitive people living in close proximity of civilised society but not joining civilisation, and not so busy in settling disputes among members of civilised society. India during that time did not require precisely formulated rules covering human behaviour relating to property in different situations. Just general description of legal formalities was sufficient unlike in other lands and civilisations where more precise legal rules were required to regulate human behavior in different situations in connection to property as they experienced advanced material civilisation with large number of articles, which gave rise to many features absent in India. Really not much evidence is available in India to indicate legal system unlike in other civilisations. The complaint is not wrong that there was no legal system or was in its primary form in ancient India in the absence of private property or in a situation of low volume of property and limited number of articles.

(4)

Division of profession happened and mankind became aware of idea of private property as a result of increase in number of artificial articles of consumption. Legal system was created to settle disputes among men in relation to possession and use of private property. We can learn that legal system was in force in all ancient civilisations if we inquire in history of law. Their written and material evidences still exist. We can not only find written evidences of legal system of comparatively young Greece and Rome but also get clear idea of it in far older Egypt, such as the kingdom was divided in 33 Namos. Local judges were there in every Namos and principal city. There was even a supreme court comprising of 30 judges. Ten judges used to be selected from each of three principal cities of Egypt, Thebes, Memphis and Onn, for appointment in Supreme Court, one among them used to be selected as chief justice. Written complaints or applications used to be lodged in courts of Egypt as it is done these days, witnesses of both complainants and defendants used to be examined, and courts used to reach conclusion and pronounce verdict based on decision of majority. Large volume of evidences of legal system in Babylon

Assyria everywhere still exists, large numbers of earthen tablets inscribed with legal edicts have been found. No one questions establishment of legal system in these civilisations. But there is no end to mystery about origin of law among mankind. Some persons complain that Royal Geographic Society did not excavate earth to find origin of law. Some other persons maintain that man is social creature by nature, everyone needs others for self protection, and law was initiated from there. Law regulates man to behave in social way, while living in community, so that no injury is inflicted by any member on other members of community. Such laws may not remain present in written form to remind mankind to behave in legal manner which is sociable also, but such unwritten rules are known to all members of mankind from beginning of existence of man on earth, and they follow such rules while living in society. Man does not need law when alone, he can do whatever he likes. One need not go very far to realize what happens to man without rule by law; it can be realized by noticing wild creatures. A lion does not target a prey which is equally strong or stronger than it, rather it targets a weaker prey. According to Sigmund Froyed attacking tendency is normal and congenital feature among mankind. All people always want to fulfill their concealed desire to attack, and for that he is ready even to attack his neighbor, grab his wealth, injure and insult him and finally to kill him inflicting pain. This attacking and cruel tendency of man remains silent waiting for opportunity and it becomes exposed with provocation by certain incidents. Fights battles murders among human groups are other expressions of this unprincipled attacking desire. Law was created to tame this congenital but concealed attacking desire of man. Human behaviour without law is comparable with that of wild beast, so it was required to establish rule of law to nurture humanity in man. Different scholars have in this way tried to explain origin of law. Even Aristotle, during golden period of Athens wrote about law — "If all people are like friends, then there is no requirement of legal prosecution". Probably he wanted to indicate that people by nature are not friendly to all and one does harm to others if he finds opportunity, and law was created to control such attacking intention of man. Human behaviour, in which humanity is not nurtured, is like that of an uncontrolled beast if it is not regulated and bridled by law.

No scholar ever discussed about where and when law was initiated, probably because it is not possible, though different scholars have tried to explain its origin in different manner. Because origin of law is rooted in distant past which was prehistoric and has no written account. That law which was initially circulated among humankind to regulate human behaviour was unwritten and mankind followed such unwritten rules for a long time before reducing rules in written form. But that could happen only after inventing alphabets and writing system. Languages appeared long before inventing writing system, we can find languages among primitive people, but they may not have writing system as it was not invented among them. We do not find origin of law, as initially law was formulated, in a time when script was not invented to record it in written form, to guide human behaviour to promote him from beastly nature to human nature, as otherwise man is beastlike in nature. But one particular idea becomes clear from writings of all scholars, all writers are unanimous that men behave in controlled and legal manner because rule by law is established, otherwise man is by nature unruly. There is a congenital brutal nature in man which finds expression at any time, which creates destruction and disturbance in human society. Man behaves in legally approved manner as it is regulated by law, otherwise man is cruel and uncontrolled like beast. Man realises his humanity while behaving according to law, otherwise he is beast. Few persons somewhere in distant past realised that humanity remains hidden under brutal and beastly instinct. But that humanity does not expose and develop voluntarily. Beastly tendency has to be thwarted to expose humanity. Humanity does not wake up, man does not find motivation to join in high thought, and cruel tendency remains so powerful and overwhelming in him that he always tends to hit others and snatch their belongings as long as animal instinct remains dominant in him.

Why do we become eager to control beastly tendency in human being if that be natural instinct in man? Natural instinct of bird is to sing with sweet note, will there appear a higher and better birdlike creature if that natural instinct is thwarted? Natural tendency of lion is to prey with tooth and claw, will there arise a higher lion like attitude if that tendency is prevented? But we have presumed that few persons somewhere realised that humanity can grow in man by restraining cruel nature in him. So there are two opposite natures in man, one is cruel and another is humane. We do not know whether anywhere few birds or lions ever came to realise whether higher birdlike or lion like instincts can be developed among them, or whether two opposing natures are there among them. Bird society or lion society can suggest and adopt suitable means to reach that higher stage if they come to learn about that. It is at least clear to us that all people do not realise about hidden humanity under beastly nature. Most of the people are driven by their cruel tendency. Or is it the fact that all people can realise and differentiate between humane and beastly natures from very beginning of existence of mankind on earth, and it is an all time and continuous endeavourr of all to nurture humane nature by subduing beastly nature? If that be so, is there any requirement of any extra law to remind and guide man always to behave humanly rejecting beastly nature, even if that law be unwritten, because in that case realization of difference between human and beastly natures is very much part of human knowledge? Suppose we consume things which are known as food and we do not consume mud and stone. Is there any requirement of any extra law relating to food intake by which man can recognize and differentiate between food and non food? It is part of basic knowledge of mankind by which a man can recognize food and activate himself to select and consume it rejecting non food. Similarly all people would join exercise to arouse humanity among them stifling beastly nature if all of them would realise by own capacity two opposing natures, this realization would be very much part of their basic knowledge, and there would be no requirement to compile an extra branch of knowledge called law to always remind man about existence of beastly nature in him and to restrain it. This exercise would be part of normal human activity. All would join voluntarily to attain humanity. There might not arise any requirement to create an extra branch called law even if not all people but at least 30 percent people would realise higher humanity in them and engage themselves to attain that, so that we could expect that rest of the people would find inspiration from them to join exercise to attain higher humanity. But that did not happen and only few persons somewhere realised humanity and felt urge to tell it to mankind. They realised that higher humanity could be attained by restraining animal instinct. It is not possible to reach higher stage of humanity as long as animal instinct remains dominant, and man remains cruel till that time. Knowledge called law was formulated as recommended by those few persons who realised higher humanity. So we have to learn where few men found exposure of knowledge and they realised higher humanity if we intend to search and find origin of law. There lies root of law. But it is extremely difficult to find that origin, because there is no written account nor is there any evidence about where in distant past and prehistoric time only few persons realised of higher humanity; so it is virtually impossible.

But here there is a huge dispute. According to these scholars origin of law is hidden in basic human instincts, as law was created to restrain such instincts. This theory presupposes that cruelty is congenital instinct in creature called man. Man is first cruel and tends to do harm to others at all time in all situations. So man is first cruel and is not hesitant to exhibit that congenital instinct and then comes humanity and knowledge called law in that order. There are many primitive groups of people living at different places on earth among whom civilisation has not progressed and who still remain in primitive condition. Population does not increase among them and they are not aware of idea of private property. They are all living peacefully as group. They distribute all food articles, whatever they collect, equally among themselves, and it is customary among them to divide equally among themselves few number of articles whatever are produced, so there is no difference in wealth or position in society. And they are all living peacefully. Then how is it proved that man exhibits his cruel nature in all situations? There did not happen frequent fights and battles everywhere among mankind when he was in primitive condition, before initiation of civilisation, though there was no education among them nor was there any division like high and low. Living evidence of primitive people, how they continue to remain on earth, is still there, noticing which we can learn about lifestyle of primitive people in distant past when all over the world people were primitive. Also Europeans did not record incidents like frequent battles among groups of primitive people when they reached within close vicinity of such people within last few centuries in different continents. The English and Portuguese captured lands in north and south America which were till that time full of jungle inhabited by primitive people. Some of the early adventurers among the English and Portuguese wrote chronicle of their experience in both of Americas, people inhabiting there and their social custom. But nowhere did they mention about frequent battles among groups of primitive people or human sacrifice in religious festivities (rather human sacrifice in religious festivals was customary at some places among civilised groups of Americas. Sculptures used for decorating temples among civilised people in Americas indicate human sacrifice). Similarly European invaders and settlers in African countries south of Sahara, where no civilisation ever appeared and all people living there were primitive, in last few centuries did not notice frequent battles among primitive people. Similar was experience of the English settlers in the Australia. We can form our opinion about lifestyle of primitive people in distant past during formation of law, noticing social behaviour of such people during last few centuries. Everywhere man used to live peacefully before start of civilisation when he was in primitive condition as he continues to live even now wherever such people still live on earth. And it is doubtful whether men would live as groups would congenital instinct of cruelty be so powerful that it would overpower all other finer human qualities. Then probably men would live separately and alone. It is true that man has become united in groups for his own interest, for self defense, for preying animals and collecting regular essential articles. But it is not possible to live in groups without fellow filling and sympathy. Possible reason for exhibition of cruelty whatever we find among mankind in these days may be difference in wealth, high and low position in society, and added with that, population increase, for which sufficient quantity of materials is not produced to meet demand of all and many people fail to collect required materials. Reason for difference in wealth position in society among mankind is production and distribution of large number of articles and creation of awareness of idea of private property, but all people do not become equally successful in production and business and collection of wealth. And population increase is also another feature and result of production of large number of articles. Population increases in countries where works are dependent on physical labour for which women are unable to join work and be dependent on men for economic reason and patriarchy appears. It happened in the past also in same order. In future large number of women will find accommodation in workshops in such countries, they will achieve economic freedom, patriarchy will vanish from society and population increase will come to a halt when works in such countries will be automated for which requirement of application of physical strength to perform jobs will end. We notice in our contemporary world that rate of increase of population in many countries is low, and in few other countries it is negative, so population in those countries is reducing. We can notice large number of women remaining engaged in jobs in these countries if we be little inquisitive. Large numbers of women there are engaged even in factories. And that has been possible because of large scale automation of works for which there is no more requirement of application of physical strength. Now works can be performed by pushing a button or handle to operate machine whereas the same job used to be performed by application of physical strength in the past before automation. Large numbers of women in those countries have found opportunity to join jobs in this new method of performing jobs, they have attained economic liberty, patriarchy has vanished and rate of increase in population has reduced. But population was continuously increasing in same countries in the past as long as works used to be performed by application of muscle power, women were unable to join jobs and patriarchy was dominant social custom as men only had capability to join jobs. Again we do not find population increase among primitive people whoever is still living, though no education is circulated among them, as subject matters of education were not found among them. Primitive people, among whom there is no education, do not show tendency to increase population; also this tendency is absent among most modern nations among whom works are all mechanised though everybody among them are educated and there is no ill educated person among them. We can reach conclusion, noticing these facts, that there is no relation between spread of education and reduction in rate of increase in population. Large numbers of articles are not in vogue among primitive people, they could not find articles as knowledge of number system was not revealed among them. They produce few numbers of articles, which are in circulation among them, using their basic instincts and intuition, and all people become able to learn production processes of these many articles. All people of society join to produce these many articles and divide produced articles equally among themselves, even women of their society take part in jobs and are entitled to claim equal share in articles along with men, and are not helplessly dependant on men. Large numbers of articles are not created, division of profession do not appear, people are not aware of idea of private property, patriarchal system is not a dominant force as women join jobs in large number and population does not increase. Again population does not increase in those highly modern and industrially advanced countries where works are automated, for which it has been possible for large number of women to join jobs, they have attained their economic freedom and independence for which dominance of patriarchy in society has vanished. Patriarchal dominance is then reason for population increase, not spread of education or absence of it. Population has increased in those civilized societies which are in intermediate stage, where large numbers of articles have been invented and produced for which jobs in production professions are heavy which disallows women to take part in works, division of profession and private property have appeared, but it has not been possible for large number of women to join jobs as they do not find situation in workshops conducive for joining on account of physically laborious nature of jobs where jobs are not automated, they lose economic liberty and helplessly accept dominance by men for which patriarchy gets upper hand. Population increases continuously in countries where works are non mechanised and dependant on physical force where women are unable to join jobs. Sufficient quantity of materials is not produced in such countries to meet total demand of population. Many people fail to earn qualities to join profession as a result of population increase, as many persons remain unsuccessful in profession and do not earn sufficient income to attain qualities. Large numbers of people in such countries remain unemployed on account of increase in population as present job market is unable to accommodate all people. Supply of prospective workers is much more than number of jobs available. Employers take opportunity of this large supply of workers to employ them at low wage. Equitable distribution of income is not accepted practice in such countries. This again in turn places obstacle before persons to attain professional qualities. Many people do not earn sufficient income as they become unsuccessful in their profession and cannot collect sufficient quantity of articles as per their demand and take resort to cruelty. There was always difference between volume of produced articles and that demanded in last many millenniums when population increased as patriarchy was in force in all civilised nations which progressed materially. Civilised people introduced administration and formulated law at initiation of division of profession when members of communities were involved in conflicts to claim possession on properties. Initially conflicts relating to property were less in number and not serious in proportion when number of articles was still few, as all people were more or less successful in profession as works in professions were light and easy to perform, though there appeared division of profession and idea of private property. Cruelty for getting possession on property did not find expression in serious proportion, and administration and legal system were equally loose without stringent measures. But gradually number of articles increased, works in professions became heavier and difficult along with that when many people failed in professions to take resort to cruelty, and administration and legal system with stringent measures were introduced to contain cruelty. There we find that cruelty found its expression when number of articles increased, people divided among many professions to produce different articles, age old custom of equal distribution of produced articles was discontinued when everyone was required to select his own profession to produce articles and to collect required materials in exchange of own produced articles and many people became unsuccessful in profession and failed to collect required materials. People were somewhat peaceful when number of articles was few and all people used to produce unitedly and there was equal distribution of articles. Nobody felt need of legal system as there was no conflict and cruelty. Even now we find absence of incidents like theft and robbery in existing primitive societies. Also population did not increase during that time, population pressure was absent on articles, people were not forced to be involved in dispute to get possession of property as volume of articles produced was sufficient to meet demand of society. We should enquire among primitive people whether they require legal system, even if it be unwritten, to contain their cruel intention. We believe law and legal system was introduced on division of profession as a result of increase in number of articles when people became aware of idea of private property and were eager to get possession of property even by force. Such people or nations used to recruit large number of their people to unite them under military force to attack and plunder some other civilised nation. This exhibition of highest form cruelty happened with large increase in number of articles when population also increased. Such difference will continue as long as population will continue to increase for patriarchal dominance in a situation of laborious nature of works. It is true that we find expression of cruelty in countries, where works are automated and population has come to a halt as large numbers of women there are engaged in jobs and patriarchy has vanished, but not because deficiency of produced articles compared to demand. Sufficient quantity of articles are produced there to meet demand of total population, but many people fail to earn income as they become unsuccessful to attain professional qualities to join job market to find accommodation in production distribution cycle of articles for varieties of reason not just related to economy or money, and they join underworld to acquire required articles even by illegal means. Still we believe number of crimes or expression of cruelty committed in highly mechanised countries relating to consumable articles is far less compared to that in non mechanised countries which are overburdened with population, large number of whom are poor whose demands remain unsatisfied. Large number of women in future will join jobs, patriarchy will vanish and population increase will reduce, most of the people will achieve success in their professions and they will not take resort to cruelty to collect required materials and consequently number of crimes will reduce as a result of large scale introduction of machines in jobs in countries where presently jobs are non mechanised and dependent on physical force, participation of women in jobs is less, patriarchy is dominant force in society, population increase is unchecked and many people take resort to cruelty to collect required material as they remain unsuccessful in their profession. And war and battle which is ultimate expression of cruelty among mankind is one of the results of population increase. If number of crimes increases and decreases with similar trend in pressure of population on property, then it can be concluded with certainty that law did not originate from endeavour to contain cruel passion. Because if origin of law would be the intention to restrain cruel passion, In that case number or proportion of crimes to total population would remain same irrespective of increase or decrease in population. Cruelty would be exhibited in same proportion by people in industrially advanced countries where population has come down as a result of introduction of large scale automation. But such countries are free from crimes to a great extent. Origin of law can be found in increase in number of articles.

Many people like to believe that changes in custom and habit of people in a country or nation happen with time and by inbuilt force of such changes according to design of certain supernatural power, when time is ripe for introduction of the change. It is beyond human capability to make any change a possibility. According to these people, difference in culture and custom among nations is the handiwork of some such invisible power, as the world is his workshop, and human beings have nothing to do in accepting or denying such custom. They are silent followers of dictums issued and customs introduced by this guiding power. Yet some other persons maintain that cultures and customs are manmade and in many cases groups of people enforce certain customs by forceful manner like agitation, revolution etc. So the reason behind different customs in different nations is that some nations agitated to forcefully propagate and introduce certain customs, while others are yet to do that. Both these groups of people fail to notice the correlation between work culture in a nation and its customs and habits of people. Peoples exhibit or follow similar culture and custom with same level of work culture when they invent and produce similar articles. Now a day there is a huge controversy worldwide regarding daring attitude and appearance of women of some countries. People of other countries, particularly those of third world, denounce women of advanced countries for their contemptible attitude, but do not observe level of work culture advanced countries have reached. Similarly many other people in third world countries agitate to liberate women of their countries, being inspired by freedom enjoyed by women in advanced countries, or to cover entire population within literacy program, as they believe that such national characteristics are achievable by agitation and enacting laws, even without automation of jobs.

Division of profession appeared among mankind as a result of increase in number of articles when everybody was unable to learn production processes of all articles. All men used to produce unitedly few numbers of articles which were in vogue in society and divide those equally among themselves. Nobody used to face difficulty or fail to learn production processes of few numbers of articles. Everybody used to possess same wealth, there was no more or less in possessed wealth or high and low in social position. But number of articles was not stagnant at any particular stage, that was increasing continuously, though this increase did not happen in few days. That time during initial stage of civilisation, few centuries used to pass for increase in number of articles. Division of profession happened when number of articles increased to cross threshold which could allow people to know production processes of all articles to work conjointly, and it was beyond capacity of any person with normal capacity to learn production processes and take part in production of all articles. All these days all people used to produce all articles unitedly and divide those equally among themselves and nobody was aware of idea of private property. But now everybody was required to select his own profession on account of division of profession as a result of increase in number of articles and society had no say in that selection process; similarly society could not determine volume of materials to be produced in individual professions and volume of other materials collected in exchange of own produced articles and it became a subject of individual decision. So idea of private property came into being just on division of profession. Everybody used to be successful in that initial stage of division of profession in some or other profession and problem of population increase did not yet start. Number of articles was still less in that initial stage of division of profession and consequently volume of articles to be produced by each producer was low as that could be sufficient to enable him to collect other articles in vogue which were few in number. Rather jobs in professions were still light. Women were still able to join in such light jobs, they had participation in economic jobs and were not thoroughly dependent on others. It was possible for women to join in few light professions like cultivation, collection of food articles and animal husbandry. Of course number of professions in those days was also very few. Dominant form of patriarchy did not appear just on division of profession, women were still not helpless. Men could not enforce their claim on women just on creating few artificial articles above threshold limit to allow them to work conjointly. Man did not feel urge to be civilized till that time, all people used to earn success in few number of professions which used to be pursued by people, population increase did not start, patriarchy did not appear and there was not much difference in possessed wealth of people though idea of private property was known as a result of division of profession, everybody used to achieve success in their own profession to collect almost equal wealth and there did not appear difference of high and low in society in terms of possession of wealth. Urge to be civilized to keep distance with lower class people was not yet felt as there was no lower strata in society till that time, everybody was more or less equally successful in collection and accumulation of wealth and nobody was unsuccessful and compelled to work in workshop belonging to others, cover with cloth was not initiated, its requirement was not felt till that time, profession of weaving did not start. Number of artificial articles was still increasing, and at certain point of time jobs in each profession became heavy. Also number of professions increased with increase in number of articles. Works in professions were light as long as number of articles was low, when each producer was required to produce low volume of articles to collect other articles. But jobs in same workshops became heavier when number of articles increased to press producers to produce more to collect other articles. That was a period of work with muscle power, mechanization of job was not a possibility even in dream, men had to perform jobs with hands and feet. Women became incapable to join jobs when jobs in professions became heavy in that period of doing jobs with muscle power. Women became dependant on men for economic reason and that was beginning of patriarchy. Men became entitled to all properties and women were denied right on property. Population started increasing as women had no power to oppose. Many persons were unsuccessful to learn professions for population increase and they joined professions of other successful businessmen as workers with fixed remuneration. By that time profit and loss in business was approved in society. A producer alone cannot produce large volume of articles, but volume of produced articles can be multiplied with the help of some employees. Owners of professions earned higher profit by selling increased volume of articles in market, and their earned wealth was also multiplied. Now society decided that earned wealth of any man would be inherited by his own children. Patriarchy became dominant force earlier, women lost right on property, now shame was imposed on women and they were confined in rooms to ensure own children of men. But men started feeling curiosity about women after confining them behind door and they forgot why and in what situation women were confined. On the one hand patriarchy was dominant social custom and men had unquestioned right on women and on the other hand they used to feel curiosity about women, added result of these two forces was rapid increase in population. Disputes among men arose relating to private property for population increase when many people failed to earn success in their own profession and were unable to collect required material in sufficient quantity, and population pressure on limited volume of articles increased. Kinds of disputes which we find in court under trial in these days relating to land of dwelling house, agricultural land, inheritance on earned wealth, share in wealth etc were all there in the past. Such disputes were created particularly for population increase when there appeared deficiency in wealth like land, house, cattle etc. Previously all persons were successful in professions and could collect required materials in sufficient quantities, though division of profession happened and men became aware of idea of private property, when number of articles increased but was few, patriarchy in dominant form did not appear as women were still able to find accommodation in workplaces and population did not increase. Sufficient quantity of materials to satisfy total demand of society used to be produced as there was no population increase. Administration with stringent measures to keep antisocial activities under control was not felt to be established as long as there were not frequent and many disputes among members of society relating to private property; but now there appeared deficiency in essential articles for increase in population, population pressure on produced articles increased and cruelty was exposed among men for collection of articles as there happened disputes relating to private property. Men became eager to set up administration with stringent measures to settle such disputes. Many of those, who became unsuccessful in their professions, when works in professions became heavy and difficult as a result of increase in number of articles, joined antisocial activities like theft robbery snatching etc. Men felt need to set up administration to protect their property from hands of such antisocial. Men were propelled to set up administration on account of increase in number of articles when patriarchy became dominant and population increased, so that pressure of population on produced articles increased which added to deficiency of and disputes relating to property. Such features became prominent among all human groups where civilisation initiated and progressed. Human societies were very small and everyone used to know others when men first felt to establish administration. First administrators among men were all elected. There used to be no problem to hold election in small human groups. None of these elected administrators used to remain in power for generations and no particular rights and facilities were considered for them. Population was increasing when number of articles increased but there were vast jungles surrounding habitats of small human groups as civilisation initiated and progressed everywhere from that stage when men were still primitive, such lands were cleared of jungles to make room for excess population and to make it suitable for cultivation, and area inhabited by men was widening, such habitats converted from village to town, town to small city, small city to large city. All city states of world – Babylon, Urr, Akkad, Athens, Sparta, Rome, Memphis – wherever education was circulated among men, large number of articles were created, patriarchy appeared and population increased, were promoted from village to city in this manner. There was no difficulty in electing administrators as long as human habitats were village or small town where everybody used to know others. Inhabitants of villages and town used to apply their franchise to elect representatives being fully informed of candidates joining fray of election. But it became a problem when villages and towns increased in population and area to become cities. It was virtually impossible during that prehistoric time to conduct a comprehensive program like election in a widespread area by determining voting centers, making arrangement of security, collecting votes of electors, counting votes to determine elected candidates getting majority of votes etc. But administrative machinery and protection were required round the clock as miscreants did not follow particular time to commit crimes. There appeared kings and dictators in the scene when villages and towns became very large to take the form of cities where it was difficult, virtually impossible, to elect representative administrators. Many businesses were created in cities by that time and some businessmen earned profuse wealth in their businesses or production and sale by employing many persons who were unsuccessful in their own professions. They were widely known in entire city as wealthy businessmen. Certain persons of some such wealthy business families formed teams of security personnel by spending some amount from their accumulated money to take over administration of cities and declared themselves as rulers or kings. Or it was also quite possible that leaders or commanders of security forces in cities declared themselves as rulers taking opportunity of difficulties to hold elections to elect administrators or disorderly conditions when villages-towns became bigger in area as cities. Royalty or rule by king appeared when villages-towns became bigger in population and area to take shape of cities where it was difficult or virtually impossible to hold election to elect administrators. Population increase did not stop after emergence of royalty and sufficient materials were not produced to meet demand of increased population. Also equitable distribution of income was not usual practice as many employers used to take advantage of greater supply of workers in job market than number of jobs available as a result of population increase, and used to employ workers at low salary. Volume of articles and lands cannot be increased to any extent at any time to meet demand of people. Also land has to be cleared by removing jungle cover and leveled to make it suitable for accommodation of excess population and cultivation when population increases. There used to appear deficiency in essential articles, men could not collect sufficient quantity of materials, and prices of materials used to rise unfairly which led to increase in incidents of theft robbery etc in city states on account of population increase. Then king of state used to unite large number of people under umbrella of military force to attack some other civilized state with intention to plunder. All wars in ancient world did not happen to satisfy aspiration of kings. All kings were not as ambitious as the great Alexander; all did not aspire to be remembered as great warriors and commanders. These wars happened for population increase. Now royalty has ended in most countries in the world, democracy has been established, but population increase has been happening unabated. Wars among countries happen even now for same reason - population increase. But some countries in the world are uniting at the same time. Requirement of application of muscle power in performing jobs has ended in European countries for large scale automation and it was possible for women to take part in jobs. Women comprise near about 50 percent of workers in such countries. Women in such countries are liberated, patriarchy has disappeared and along with that population increase has reduced, it is negative in some countries. All people are educated in such countries, it is not possible to find accommodation in mechanised system of work without education and skill. Earnest intention of people of these countries found expression in united coexistence. No more they intend to battle among themselves. European countries are uniting to form one country. Already they have reached agreement to introduce common customs, such as legal tender money to ease transactions in business, unrestricted movement of men and materials, certain common rules eliminating local prohibitive rules etc. it can be expected that they will introduce common custom in many other areas in near future like military force. But same countries were engaged in battles in the past on account of varieties of differences and disputes which snowballed two times into world war when jobs in such countries were non mechanised and there used to exist large number of ill educated people to perform jobs, women could not join jobs for requirement of muscle power in jobs and patriarchy was dominant social custom and there was large scale population increase in countries. Therefore we find that exhibition of cruelty among mankind has been happening in connection with articles of consumption which do not remain easily and equally accessible to all people when population increases. There was no expression of cruelty among primitive people as long as there were few numbers of articles and equal distribution of articles. And population increase is also an outcome of increase in number of articles when works in professions become heavy as every producer is required to produce large volume of articles, and works are done with manual labour for which women are expelled from work places. System of administration and legal system were introduced to settle disputes among mankind relating to property. System of administration changes from elected community leaders to royalty and then autocracy or democracy but disputes among mankind remain unchanged and unending as long as population increases and many people remain unsuccessful to earn sufficient income to collect required materials. Exhibition of crimes and cruelty in various forms like theft, robbery, murder and highest of them all, war, continue to happen. But same nations which were once engaged in wars in the past are now showing lesser inclination to wars when jobs in their countries are mechanised as a result of advancement of science technology, where large number of women have found accommodation in workplaces and achieved economic liberty. Population increase in such countries has come to a halt and they are now uniting instead of warring among themselves. Other crimes are also much less in number in such countries, as most of the people are successful in collecting required materials, in proportion to number of population as compared to number of crimes committed in countries inhabited by large number of ill educated people where population increase is unchecked. Such turns of events hardly prove that legal system originated from cruel passion in man. Would it originate so, then number of crimes in proportion to number of population would remain same irrespective of spread of education or not or population increase or not, because man would always in all situation would exhibit same propensity to cruelty. Cruelty did not find rampant exposure when man was primitive, and its incidents reduce when jobs become automated. It remained or remains in large proportion during intermediate period as long as articles are many and jobs are labour intensive.

But introduction of automation in workplaces to repel muscle power for performing jobs, so that women can get opportunity to join jobs so that population is reduced and incidents of crimes are also reduced, is not an easy task. It is an unwritten rule among mankind that only ill educated people show eagerness to perform non mechanised and physically laborious jobs and educated people do not join such jobs as long as such jobs remain so anywhere in the world. This unwritten rule is in force irrespective of difference of land, period, religion, language or nation. A large band of ill educated people live in society to perform jobs as long as such jobs remain physically laborious, but educated people join same jobs when such jobs become mechanised, and heavy and laborious parts of jobs are performed mechanically. Ill educated people exclusively remain engaged in agriculture as long as it remains dependant on ordinary ploughing machine, hoe, sickle etc. and educated people do not show eagerness to join agricultural profession. Educated people at best remain involved in agricultural operation in the capacity of owners of land or joining in trade of agricultural produce. History of automation of jobs is not very old, it started from beginning of twentieth century when jobs could be performed by mechanical power in place of muscle power. Before that machines which were installed in workplaces belonged to primary or certain intermediate stage and muscle power wsas required to operate them. Hoe, axe are also machine but of primary stage and are operated by application of muscle power. Works were non mechanised and dependant on muscle power before twentieth century but history of education and educational institutions is very old. Did we ever notice any person qualified from Delhi, Bombay or Calcutta University cultivating land with ploughing machine and hoe? But many educated boys and girls eagerly joined cultivation when labour eliminating machines like tractors, harvesters, sprayers etc were introduced in this job. Similarly ill educated people remained engaged with means of transport as long as mediums or components of transportation were palanquin, rickshaw, horse drawn cart etc and no educated people used to be engaged in that job. But many educated boys and girls eagerly joined such jobs when airplane, train, motor car, bus etc. were introduced. Nobody knows why mankind behaves this way but it is an unwritten rule of mankind and a common feature of entire humankind of the world. Labour eliminating machines appeared more or less from beginning of twentieth century, works in all countries before that were muscle power dependant, but mechanization of jobs did not take place in all countries of the world simultaneously in same rate of advancement from beginning of twentieth century. There are many countries in the world which are known as third world countries where works are non mechanised labour dependant even in these days. A large band of ill educated people remain in any country to perform labour dependant jobs whenever and wherever jobs remain so. Works in such countries are fit to be performed exclusively by men for labour intensive nature and women have no participation in jobs, patriarchy is dominant and population is ever increasing. Requirement of physical strength has ended as a result of large scale proliferation of automation in jobs, educated people now eagerly join jobs and even women work in association with and side by side to men in countries which are inhabited only by educated people and are considered as first rated, and most advanced and improved. All people in such countries are educated, prospect of finding accommodation without education and skill in mechanised system of performance is bleak. Also educated people show eagerness to perform jobs with labour eliminating machines. Patriarchy has vanished and population is low as a direct outcome of large scale participation of women in jobs. But these highly mechanised and first rated countries of today were non mechanised, before large scale mechanization or before twentieth century, when machines for mechanization were not available as those were not yet invented. Labour eliminating machines were not yet invented but jobs must be accomplished. Machines, which were in use in such countries during that period, were not fully labour eliminating, or muscle power was required to operate machines to accomplish jobs. A huge army of ill educated people used to be present in country to perform such jobs. It is absolutely wrong to think that people of such countries have always been educated from distant past noticing all pervading education now in such countries. Patriarchy was firmly aground in these countries and these were overburdened with population pressure when works were labour intensive there. Then frequent wars used to break out among such countries and large number of people used to perish. Many battles took place among European countries till end of nineteenth century even if we do not take into consideration two world wars of twentieth century as if these were abnormal. But today such countries are intending to remain unitedly; education has become all pervading for large scale automation of jobs, patriarchy has vanished because of widening of opportunities for women to join jobs in large scale and population increase has been lowered. This intention of coexistence is exhibition of earnest desire of all educated people of these countries, they no more want wars, rather peaceful cohabitation is their sincere wish. Population increased in large scale in European countries as long as works there were non mechanised labour intensive; and European nations proliferated and dispersed in the world most in last few centuries, even they captured few continents by virtue of sheer huge number. European nations increased in number by more than 500 percent in last few centuries. We do not know whether inhabitants of Americas, Australia, new Zeeland and South Africa are included in it or not; if they were not taken into consideration, then Europeans increased at least by 2000 percent. Whereas to our surprise Africans increased least, some 40 percent, during same period till middle of twentieth century.

Education is widespread and population increase is low in some countries of the world, particularly in European and North American countries. This has been possible by automation of jobs or for introducing labour eliminating machines in jobs. These countries had to invent labour repealing machines. Scientific and technical knowledge has to progress for invention and development of machine. Probably scientists and technicians observed that large volume of jobs could be performed far more speedily and by employing lesser number of men if jobs are done with the help of machines, or larger volume of jobs could be performed with lower cost in lesser time. These machines are modern day version of hammer, hoe, pick axe, digging rod etc. of the past. It is possible to perform same kind of jobs with lathe, grinding, milling etc. machines what could be done with hammer, hoe etc. Hammer, hoe, pick axe etc are machines of the past whose application requires muscle power; lathe, grinding etc. are modern versions of machines of the past which require very low application of muscle power; though all these are commonly known as machine. Both old and modern machines can perform same nature of jobs like breaking, boring, smoothening, turning, lifting etc. Modern machines can be operated by pushing a handle, circulating a steering or pressing a button and jobs can be performed. Development of machine will not stop at stage where it has reached today. Scientists and technicians are engaged in different countries of the world to invent and develop machines. In future works will be performed by remote control system or robots just by pressing buttons, while remaining sitting in home or office, with the help of higher improved machines which are going to be invented and introduced. Then machines will operate according to premeditated program designed by computer. Men will only press buttons of computers sitting in office or home and machines will operate in shop floors of factories, on roads and fields. Then at that time also much higher improved machines will be called machines and their operation will require much less application of physical labour than what it is today. Some persons who were engaged with jobs in workshops in last few centuries noticed that less number of people were required and larger volume of products could be produced in much lesser time with the help of machines. A lathe machine can cut into pieces as many iron rods as can be done by 20 or more persons in a certain time span. But one or two persons are sufficient to operate a lathe machine. Such features of producing larger volume of products in less time, employing less number of men and spending less money inspired businessmen and producers to invent and introduce machines. Physical force was required to operate machines during many stages of development of machines and ill educated people were engaged with operation of machines at such stages. It was found at certain stage that physical strength was no more required to operate machines and educated people became interested to do that job. For example printing machine for a long time after being invented by Gutenberg and for many stages during its development was labour intensive and only ill educated people used to show eagerness to work with machine. Now printing machine has reached certain stage of development where requirement of physical strength is no more to operate it and educated persons show interest to work with machine. Physical strength was required to operate rail engine when George Stevenson invented it and thereafter for a long time during many stages of development of it. Now the machine has reached certain stage of development when physical strength is no more required to operate it.

There used to be no ambitious plan program to develop science technology in the past when royalty or rule by king was order of the day in the whole world. Kings did not use to show much interest in development of science technology. They were more eager to spend for royal amusement. Of course one reason for lack of interest in development of science technology was absence of knowledge that production and distribution of artificial articles were at the root of creation and continuous run of civilized society; division of profession, awareness of idea of private property, difference in wealth, initiation of administration all appeared as a result of invention and production of artificial articles; and science technology targets to invent and develop those artificial articles.

This idea is not clear to entire humankind even in these days that all activities throughout the world have been happening as a result of invention of and business in artificial articles. All development in science technology in the past during royalty happened by private effort getting no patronage from royalty. Kings never used to show interest and spend to invent and develop any articles other than war machines though they used to impose sales tax on produced articles and that used to be main source of income for state coffer. Idea of sales tax is nothing new in the world, it has been followed from ancient time. Production and sale of artificial articles could contribute sales tax to state coffer which could increase state income if new articles would be invented and developed by exercise in science technology and put to production and sale during their tenure as king. Scientific and technical exercise would not just be expensive, it would fetch revenue also to state coffer by inventing and developing new articles and putting them to production and sale. But royalties had no such comprehensive and far reaching ideas, and added to that they were more interested to spend for royal amusement. There was no well designed plan program in the whole world in those days for exercise in science technology to invent and develop new articles. Few persons somewhere felt interest to join in study of science technology and progress of it and invention and development of artificial articles happened by such individual effort during that time. Volume of subject matter to study in subjects of science technology was thin in those days and suitable for learning by individual effort as very few persons used to join study of science technology, because this exercise could not fetch income to them. Volume can be bigger if large number of people join exercise in science technology and their findings be added in the subject matter which is why such subjects are huge these days. Improvement in science technology and invention and development of articles progressed in the hands of few such persons in last few centuries when rule by king was system of administration. All those Gutenberg of printing machine fame, Leuwenhoek of lens, Stevenson of rail engine, Lavoisier of oxygen etc. invented articles by individual effort. None of them was associated with any laboratory, though Lavoisier had his private laboratory as he was a landlord and greatly rich. Most of them were associated with certain workshops for production of articles; probably they were not ill educated – machines in those days were labour intensive and only ill educated persons used to show interest to join jobs with such machines – and were engaged with administration or supervision of jobs. They noticed from close proximity that works were performed with machines in less time spending less cost. Volume of science technology was increasing by individual effort and study by few such persons somewhere. Inventors of articles used to be considered as proprietors of such articles as long as invention and development of articles happened by individual effort, as long as subject matter of science technology was thin or not very large; and either they could earn rich dividend by producing such articles in their own workshops and selling them in market, or could earn royalty by allowing some other producers to produce. Large business houses came forward to patronize science technology for its advancement when volume of subject matters of science technology became huge to cross limit of individual capacity to study it. We do not know whether they had knowledge that artificial articles were at the root of all activities, movements and hustling bustling of the world, but we believe that such large business houses at least had knowledge that articles were at the root of business. And business in articles was main target of such business houses. Such houses used to appoint teams of scientists technicians after establishing laboratories. Articles or production process invented by joint effort of such teams used to belong to the houses. Volume of science technology is increasing even now. Experiment in technology is hugely expensive and production processes of many artificial articles do not belong to even large business houses as it is beyond capacity of such large houses to join in experiment of such articles. Volume of subject matter of any branch of science technology is now of such a proportion that few persons now cannot conduct experiment on any field. A laboratory now requires to appoint many people, all of whom are experts deserving lucrative salary, for which scientific experiments are now a days so expensive. Such houses are mostly eager to develop small articles like tooth paste and brush, soap and detergent powder, plastic bottle etc. Even now experiments in large and complicated artificial articles are beyond capacity of large business houses on account of their huge expensive nature. We believe that in future volume of subject matters for experiments in small articles will become so huge and complicated that it will be beyond capacity of business houses to participate in such experiments. Then only governments of countries will conduct experiments in technology of all articles, large and small. Then study in electronics will not remain confined in such study only, it will merge with mechanical, electrical, chemical etc so intensely that subject matter to study electronics will be huge. Similar developments will happen in all other branches. Then it will be beyond capacity of business houses to conduct experiments in such branches. All experiments in articles will then be conducted by patronage only from governments, just on account of increase in volume of subject matter of any branch of science. Already at no stage large business houses ever patronized or spent liberally for experiments in fundamental science as such experiments in fundamental science is huge but do not fetch income to business houses. Production technologies are utilized for business purposes and business houses just become eager to spend to conduct experiments to determine production technologies. Fundamental experiments in science are always conducted in universities and few other institutions patronized by governments. Now we notice that experiments for development of production technologies of articles are going to be responsibilities of governments just because of increase in volume of subject matter of such science technology. Division of profession appeared for increase in number of artificial articles many millenniums ago in distant past and private property was created and administration was introduced to settle disputes relating to such properties and their protection. Administration was introduced for increase in number of articles, or in other words we can say that administration originated from artificial articles. There is no written account of creativity in mankind and gradual development of articles at initial stage during that prehistoric time. Creation and development of articles were done by individual effort for many centuries starting from that initial stage when volume of subject matter of science technology was very thin and easily comprehensible by any individual. Now we notice that study and experiment in science technology is going beyond capacity of individual persons just because of increase in volume of subject matter. Even large business houses hesitate to bear expenditure of conducting experiments in technology. Many persons are required to be appointed for experiment in any branch of science technology as any branch is intensely related with many other branches. Such persons who are appointed for conducting experiments are specialists and claimants of high remuneration, and for this reason experiments are now hugely expensive. Now we notice that a new responsibility is going to be shouldered by governments or administrative machineries. Now administrative machinery is going to take responsibility of the job from which administration was created and introduced in the world and continues to exist; jobs which are at the root of establishing administration, or creation and development of artificial articles, for sheer reason of increase in volume of subject matter of science technology.

Automation of jobs happens as a result of progress of science technology. Kings had no headache for progress of science technology in the past during royalty or rule by kings. Their thoughts were not so far fetching to think that many artificial articles could be invented and developed by progress of science technology and new businesses could be set up to do business in such articles which could contribute large income in government coffer as taxes and duties. Their only concern was huge expenditure for experiments in science technology. Of course the knowledge that artificial articles were at the root of business and even administration was not clearly known to humankind as it is not even now. All progress in science technology used to happen by individual effort. Thereafter business houses took charge of developing production technologies of articles. But business houses never showed interest in progress of fundamental science other than production technologies of articles; there is no opportunity of income from conducting experiment in fundamental science, though it is enormously expensive. Coming to this age we notice that governments are going to take responsibility for experiments in fundamental science as well as development of production technology for increase in volume of subject matter of any branch of science technology for which study and experiment in any branch is hugely expensive. We notice that some countries have progressed very far in improvement of science technology, impediments before large scale participation of educated people and women in jobs have been cleared by automation of jobs and population there is low. Also we notice many countries where there is no progress of science technology, works are labour intensive and dependant on muscle power, educated people and women have no participation in jobs and countries are disturbed with population pressure though system of administration is democracy. Governments of those countries are only interested in progress of science technology where all people are educated. We can also notice that there is no criminal among elected representatives of people in such countries inhabited by educated people only. Educated mass of countries, who are electors, regularly study mediums of news to keep themselves informed of activities of elected representatives. Antisocial activities of any elected representative find place in mediums of news and do not escape notice of electors. That representative loses his candidature and also chances to be elected in next election. Countries progress in experiments in science technology according to demand of educated electors. Political parties joining fray of election include program for spread of education and progress of science technology in their agenda judging demand of educated electors. Probably people of such countries have no clear idea that science technology target invention of new artificial articles or developing existing articles whose production and business are at the root of creation of civilized society, continuation of business and commerce and establishment of administrative machinery, but they have a common idea that experiments in science technology are ways and means of improvement and to know about nature or universe, and they feel an irrational and irresistible emotional attraction to scientific activities or study of nature; also they stress on scientific activities as part of program of spread of education. Political parties taking part in election include experiment in science technology in their agenda and commitments judging emotional attitude of people or electors towards science technology. Elected representatives determine their future program and prepare budget after joining parliament or legislative assembly. Such representatives remember their commitments before election while determining their future plan of action, and experiment in science technology is included in future plan of action; and a sizeable amount of money is kept earmarked for this program. Thereafter allocated money is utilized properly according to plan of action, and any deviation in that utilisation of allocated money is reported in news mediums and comes to the knowledge of elector people. Minister in charge for progress of science technology loses his ministry and runs the risk of expulsion from ministry. Reason for progress in science technology by advanced countries is this; there educated electors, who regularly keep their eyes on news mediums to get information of activities of ministers, supervise activities of representatives of people appointed as ministers in charge.

Contrary to this, political parties and candidates take advantage of ignorance of people or electors to include any commitment in political agenda without any intention to fulfill it in countries, inhabited largely by ill educated people who are in majority, where works are non mechanised labour intensive for which large number of uneducated people live there to perform jobs, if such countries follow democratic process to elect administrators extending voting right to all irrespective of educational level. Elector people in such countries are uneducated ignorant and are not able to keep eyes on news medium. Speeches delivered by political candidates are only means for them to know. Most of such ill educated electors live in remote villages far away from cities and city suburbs and engaged with agriculture, animal husbandry, village transportation etc jobs. Their extent of knowledge is confined within their village limits. Political parties and their leaders taking part in election deliver speeches in gatherings of such people before election. Such speeches contain political commitments of such parties which are prepared taking into consideration extent of knowledge and comprehension and likes and dislikes of such ignorant villagers.

Such political commitments include subsidy in fertilizer, subsidy in seed, in electricity, storage, transportation and many other tall commitments which village cultivators like to listen. But most parts of such political speeches contain denouncement of opposition political parties and their leaders than commitments, opposition to their activities, such as inaction by opposition parties to improve agriculture and roads in villages, corruption in village schools and hospitals etc. Possible reason for such denouncement of opposition in priority of commitment of own party may be that past records of such political parties are not very bright. Political parties and candidates who offer political speeches including therein both denouncement and commitment in bright fashion run greater chance to be victorious. Also money gets a very important place in election among ill educated villagers. Victorious candidates from village constituencies dominated by ill educated voters go to join parliaments or legislative assemblies which are mostly located in the capitals of countries and states, and do not remain in villages. Such peoples' representatives become involved in various crimes while remaining outside visible range of electors in their village constituencies. Such crimes are regularly exposed in news mediums but elected candidates with criminal disposition damn such news as illiterate electors in villages cannot read and learn such news. Elected representatives know that such news do not reach electors in villages, so his vote bank among villagers remain unaffected and unaltered. Same candidates again contest next election and deliver speeches in gatherings of illiterate villagers where they again promise bright commitments which villagers like to listen, denounce opposite political parties and their candidates and spend a part of money earned in crimes, and again become elected to join ministry. Such news about criminal activities of political leaders and ministers which are expressed in news mediums are political issues for city dwelling educated people, but not for village illiterates. A country remains largely inhabited by ill educated people if majority of jobs in such countries are performed by muscle power, and most electoral constituencies are dominated by uneducated people except few constituencies in cities and city suburbs dominated by educated people. Probably honest candidates are elected from educated electors dominated constituencies as electors there are educated and able to read and get news to judge, but their number is less and they are minority in parliaments and legislative assemblies. Majority of victorious representatives there are elected from ill educated electors dominated constituencies. Thereafter such an elected representative with criminal disposition takes charge of ministry for progress of science technology. Certain plans of action are designed and primary accounts of incomes and expenses like budgets are drawn in such countries for show before eyes of the world. There would be no loss if these were not there, because these are never fabricated with intention to be followed. Opposition parties complain that government of country has drawn no plan program and budget for improvement, and parties forming ministry claim that such things are there, but who among ill educated electors from villages have the capability to inquire to check for himself whether these are truly there or not. Their ignorance is huge block impeding them to know. These are peculiarities of election among illiterate voters. Minister in charge for ministry for improvement of science technology appoints certain persons loyal to him as principal administrators of science laboratories. All purchases and sales of machines and materials of experimental centers are administered by such chief administrators who are loyal to minister in charge. Deals for all purchases and sales are settled under the table. Suppliers supply below quality machines and materials to experimental centers. Inspiration and earnest intention to work there are spoiled. Activities which are in no way related to experiment in science technology get bigger attention in such centers. Corrupt activities of minister in charge and sympathetic chief administrators of centers are exposed in news mediums, but minister feels no headache for that, electors in his constituencies do not come to learn such corruptions, vote bank of minister among electors remains unaltered as before. But experiments in science technology in such countries do not progress, machines are not developed and automation of jobs remains a distant possibility. Jobs in such countries largely remain non automated and laborious where only ill educated people feel eager to join. Large numbers of uneducated people continue to exist in such countries. Education does not become widespread though schools and colleges are established everywhere. Rather school buildings become dilapidated being unattended and not maintained. These countries inhabited by large number of Ill educated people commit a grave mistake from very beginning, they allow franchise to all persons attaining majority in such countries irrespective of education level. Then candidates with criminal disposition are elected term after term of election, exploiting ignorance of electors, and continue with corrupt practices with impunity and countries do not progress in scientific and technical fields. They do not learn invention of new articles or labour repellant machines for automation. Many peoples' representatives with criminal record are present in parliaments and legislative assemblies in countries inhabited by large number of uneducated people. In contrast this mistake has not been committed in countries scientifically and industrially advanced. These countries were inhabited by large number of uneducated people when works there were non mechanised labour dependant. Most of such countries had royalty as system of administration at that time. Population increase was unrestricted. But franchise was not allowed to all persons in such countries attaining majority irrespective of educational level while transforming from royalty to democracy. Only educated people, who could collect news and be able to analyse for determining right candidates, were allowed franchise. Newspapers are one of the important pillars of democracy, but newspapers do not play important role in countries with large ill educated population, they do not know reading writing. They do not come to learn corrupt practices of candidates joining fray in election and candidates take that opportunity. Newspapers play important role in countries inhabited by only educated people. Peoples' representatives with criminal records were never elected in the history of parliaments and assemblies in such countries. This was possible because uneducated people who were not able to collect news and to analyse and determine were never allowed franchise in such countries at any time during course of democracy. Progress in science technology can happen only in democratic countries where franchise is strictly restricted among educated persons who can be supervisors and analysts of activities of elected representatives. Only such countries can develop and introduce machines for work in workshops so that jobs can be mechanised in which women can work. We find lesser number of incidents of crimes in such countries as population increase is low and sometimes nil. Legal systems of such countries are greatly relieved from pressure of large number of crimes committed unlike in third world countries.

Division of profession happened among mankind for increase in number of artificial articles, awareness for private property was created, system of administration was introduced, patriarchy appeared and population increased. Deficiency appear in essential articles, sufficient quantities of articles are not produced in such countries to meet total demand as a result of population increase, prices of materials increase unfairly. Besides large numbers of people do not get opportunity to be successful in their profession for population increase, they fail to collect sufficient quantity of materials as needed and become poor. Many of them join antisocial activities. Kings used to unite a large number of such excess population, mostly drawn from poor section of people, under umbrella of military force to attack other countries, when in the past there was rule by royalty everywhere; their intention was plundering. We find many countries even these days acquiring war machineries and engaged in war when royalty has been abolished from most countries and democracy has been introduced. We shall find same reason, population increase, behind all such wars if we enquire. Rate of population increase has not reduced, works in such countries are labour dependant where women are unable to join jobs and patriarchy is dominant force in society though democracy has been introduced there. Wars break out among such countries and large numbers of lives perish with regularity. Works are no longer dependant on muscle power in countries where large scale automation of works has taken place, job opportunities before women there is wide open, near about 50 percent of workers there are women, their economic liberty has been ensured, patriarchy has vanished and population increase is low, in some countries it is negative. Sufficient quantity of materials as demanded by people are produced and collected in such countries, all people are able to collect required material and not much trouble is there relating to want of materials, they do not feel need to engage in war, and peaceful coexistence is their intention. Number of people per family is low as rate of population increase is low and all people find opportunity to achieve success in professions, and number of incidence of cruelty and crime is far less. Number of incidence of cruelty and crime is low in such countries in new arrangement where population increase shows decreasing trend as a result of automation of works. Incidences of crime whatever we find in such countries happen as many boys and girls fail to attain professional qualities to join profession for which the principal reason is non economic. Incidences of crimes are far less among primitive people, practically nil, as number of articles is less, difference in wealth is absent as there is equal distribution of wealth and there is no population increase, so everyone gets sufficient quantity of articles. Subsequently as long as number of articles was low and works in professions were light, imposing patriarchy did not appear till that time, population increase did not happen as rate of increase was low and everyone used to get opportunity to achieve success in profession for a long time in the course of increase of articles though division of profession and private property appeared. Everybody used to be able to collect required quantity of materials and incidence of crime was less. We found many people who were unsuccessful in their professions, deficiency of essential articles and expression of cruelty among people during intermediate period of some thousands of years only when jobs in professions were heavy and labour intensive for which women were unable to join jobs, patriarchy was dominant social custom and population increased at fast rate. Ultimate expression of cruelty is war when many people perish. Such devastating wars come to halt as a result of automation, when population increase stops. It is disputable whether it is proper to conclude that legal system was introduced just to check passion called cruelty which, if not reined with law, is always destructive. We can probably hold that this expression of cruelty is temporary when this passion finds many vents of exposure though range of intermediate period is some thousands years when this passion is most virulent, people are involved in large number of crimes for collection of materials for consumption and states and nations are engaged in battles. Cruelty should find free vent of expression in all situations and in equal proportion should it be the reason for creation of legal system as it is presumed that it exhibits its fangs without provocation; incidences of cruelty should not reduce even among highly advanced and mechanised countries of these days where works are no more labour intensive as a result of widespread automation and population increase has reduced. We find exhibition of cruelty is low in highly mechanised countries though all boys and girls are constantly busy to attain success in private professions for which there is competitive condition among them. It is disputable to say that legal system was created to restrict cruelty to promote humanity when it is presupposed that cruelty is a basic human nature, as it is equally questionable whether cruelty exhibits itself in all situations. Rather we like to believe that disputes arose among mankind relating to private property when there appeared division of profession as a result of increase in number of artificial articles and idea of private property became known, particularly when patriarchy appeared and population increased. Law was compiled to regulate human behaviour relating to private property. Of course certain other law might be in force among mankind even before that to regulate marriage and marital relation. Root of law relating to private property is aground in distant past during prehistoric time which has neither written account nor any material evidence.

The persons, who are unable to achieve success with their own quality and capability, can take most advantage of absence of legal system. It is essential to enforce rule of law, particularly for those, who show greater eagerness to earn by virtue of own capability. But man introduces and enacts some laws, which are some kind of impediments to main activities of civilisation, under influence of wrong perception. Mankind is even now unable to realise that law was created as a result of activities of production and distribution of articles of consumption; even now mankind has wrong notion that law was originated for restraining cruel passion in man to control him for promoting his humane qualities. Some laws are enacted, for such mistaken notion, which are impediments to production and distribution. We particularly refer to taxing statutes. Taxes and duties must be there as there should exist administration for the benefit of human society. Administration was instituted among mankind for giving protection to man when there appeared many varieties of articles which gave way to division of profession and idea of private property, and which also germinated among many people intention to acquire articles by robbing and stealing. Taxes and duties must be there to run administration. There cannot be opposition to existence of administration and taxes and duties. But that does not mean that taxing statutes should enjoy greater importance than principal job of production and distribution, and such acts should be framed in complicated and incomprehensible manner so that there can be many interpretations and disputes. Such universal mistake has been committed for not giving proper importance to production and distribution. We find that legal formalities and long drawn court battles get greater importance than main activity behind human civilisation. Large numbers of people are engaged in such unproductive activities. Such legal formalities are followed as certain laws have been enacted; if the laws are not there, legal formalities will not be required. And such laws are not that important, those can be scrapped. There are some other instances where some other features of material civilisation have got greater importance than production and distribution. Money was created for ease of transaction when number of articles increased and mankind was facing trouble in exchange. Money is not like other materials of consumption. It was created not for consumption and enjoyment but just for ease of exchange. But subsequently we found many persons started accumulating money to play major role in production and distribution, even without knowing production and distribution. They are just investors but claim all profit. For them this activity became more important than production and distribution. Even then we have to keep a balance while enacting laws to see that such laws do not pose problem to production and distribution of articles – the main and central job for human civilisation.

www.ingramcontent.com/pod-product-compliance
Lightning Source LLC
Chambersburg PA
CBHW070705290526
45790CB00001B/454